Praise for

John Taylor Gatto

I count John Gatto among my heroes.

— Robert Bly

I've loved John Gatto's work ever since I first encountered his astounding essays.

— Christiane Northrup, MD, author of *Women's Bodies, Women's Wisdom*

Gatto's voice is strong and unique, a Socrates of the educational world.

— Thomas Moore, author of *Care of the Soul*

I agree with damn near every semi-colon and comma that Mr. Gatto has written.

— Tom Peters, author of *In Search of Excellence*

Gatto is a singular antidote to stale convention.

— David Guterson, author of *Snow Falling On Cedars*

A remarkable achievement. I can't remember ever reading such a profound analysis of modern education.

— Howard Zinn, on *The Underground History of American Education*

Education's most original thinker.

— Daniel H. Pink, author of *Free Agent Nation*

Brilliant Work!

— Laissez Faire Books

Good software can even be designed to emulate the most outstanding teachers in history, preserving the genius of people like John Taylor Gatto for future generations.

— Robert Epstein, PhD, Former editor, *Psychology Today*

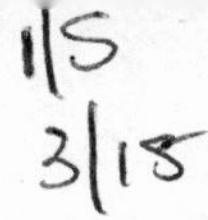

Praise for

WEAPONS OF MASS INSTRUCTION

John Taylor Gatto has been a hero of mine for years. He has the courage to challenge an educational system that is obsolete and out of touch with reality. Years ago, he gave me the courage to speak out and write my books. I trust this book will give you the courage to speak out.

— ROBERT KIYOSAKI, author of *Rich Dad, Poor Dad*

or over 20 years John Taylor Gatto has been working tirelessly to ch us the truth about our educational system — that compulsory schooling does not work to foster a democratic way of life!

— MARY LEUE, Founder of the Albany Free School

ll of Gatto's words shine. Let's have Gatto as US Secretary of Education, and then this time, he can blow it all up!

— GEORGE MEEGAN, author of *The Longest Walk* and world record holder, longest unbroken march in human history

We accept Mr. Gatto's invitation to an open conspiracy against forced schooling here in Europe as well. The virtues of this book, its precise ideas, realistic proposals and sharp conscience, class it among the best works of Thoreau, Jefferson, Hume or Diderot. A masterly book.

— *The Kadmos Paris Magazine*, Paris/October 2008

In *Weapons of Mass Instruction*, John Taylor Gatto points out the folly of the business of American education, especially standardized testing. Listen up, for children's sake!

— WENDY ZEIGLER, artist and former student of John Taylor Gatto

It happens rarely, but whenever I do read a newspaper, listen to the radio, or watch television, on a variety of topics, I find myself wondering, "How? How can this happen? How can people be so gullible?" Gatto has an answer, and it is disturbing as well as compelling: 20th Century US education. His argument renews gratitude to my father for having given me the chance to dodge full immersion in the homogenizing machine, and makes me more determined than ever to pass this gift of becoming an individual on to my own children.

—Tania Aebi, author of *Maiden Voyage* and world record holder, first circumnavigation of the world by a solo female sailor

I run a school. John Gatto is my conscience. He has taught me to hate school and love learning. This book will do that for others, and we need them!

— Becky Elder, Northfield School of The Liberal Arts

John Taylor Gatto explains how compulsory public schools train children to be employees and consumers instead of leaders and achievers in a free America.

— Phyllis Schlafly, president of Eagle Forum

John Taylor Gatto has forcefully presented the case that ... a people who believe in freedom will never emerge from a system that starts with coercion.

— Michael P. Farris Chairman, Home School Legal Defense Association

John Taylor Gatto reminds us that children aren't just a future workforce in need of training. They're individuals curious about the world, and citizens of a self-governing republic. Our decisions about education should reflect that.

—David Boaz Executive Vice President, Cato Institute, author, *Libertarianism: A Primer* and *The Politics of Freedom*

WEAPONS OF MASS INSTRUCTION

A Schoolteacher's Journey through the Dark World of Compulsory Schooling

JOHN TAYLOR GATTO

Author of the best-selling Dumbing Us Down

NEW SOCIETY PUBLISHERS

Cataloging in Publication Data:

A catalog record for this publication is available
from the National Library of Canada.

Cover design by Diane McIntosh.
Cover art: George Deem, detail of *Art School*, 1989. Oil on canvas.

Printed in Canada. Hardcover copyright ©2009 by John Taylor Gatto.

Paperback ISBN: 978-0-86571-669-8

Inquiries regarding requests to reprint all or part of *Weapons of Mass Instruction*
should be addressed to New Society Publishers at the address below.

To order directly from the publishers,
please call toll-free (North America) 1-800-567-6772,
or order online at: www.newsociety.com

Any other inquiries can be directed by mail to:

New Society Publishers
P.O. Box 189, Gabriola Island, BC V0R 1X0, Canada
(250) 247-9737

New Society Publishers' mission is to publish books that contribute in fundamental ways to building an ecologically sustainable and just society, and to do so with the least possible impact on the environment, in a manner that models this vision. We are committed to doing this not just through education, but through action. This book is one step toward ending global deforestation and climate change. It is printed on Forest Stewardship Council-certified acid-free paper that is **100% post-consumer recycled** (100% old growth forest-free), processed chlorine free, and printed with vegetable-based, low-VOC inks, with covers produced using FSC-certified stock. Additionally, New Society purchases carbon offsets based on an annual audit, operating with a carbon-neutral footprint. For further information, or to browse our full list of books and purchase securely, visit our website at: www.newsociety.com

NEW SOCIETY PUBLISHERS
www.newsociety.com

MIX
Paper from
responsible sources
FSC® C016245

Contents

A Dedication for the Family Builders

I DEDICATE THIS BOOK to the great and difficult art of family-building and to its artists, the homeschoolers in particular, but all forms represented for me by the finest family I ever saw — the Hitchons of Plymouth, England; Brantford, Canada; and Uniontown, Pennsylvania — especially in the person of my darling friend of sixty-five years, Ronald Bright Hitchon. Without Ron's constant help and advice, this book — and all my writing — would never have happened. The Hitchon Historical Archive is kept by John Hitchon of Inverberry, Scotland.

Ron and his family have been my spirit friends since I was ten, my models of transcendental excellence. His ancestor, Richard Hitchens, was lord mayor of Plymouth when the *Mayflower* sailed from its harbor; another ancestor, John Bright, was the troublemaker who helped give England free trade in 1846; his cousin, Trevor Howard, was my favorite movie actor as the lead in "*The Outcast of the Islands*," and as ferocious Lord Cardigan in *Charge of the Light Brigade*. His uncle, Louis Bauman, won the first Carnegie Medal for risking his own life to save the lives of others.

Ron's dad, Ted Hitchon, taught me algebra. His mother, Virginia Bauman, hid me when I played hooky from school (and his dog, Flicka, bit me where I hid). At Cornell, his brother Larry stood sponsor for me as a fraternity pledge. His niece, Ginny, advised me patiently on a reunion with my long-lost daughter, Briseis, in the orchid jungles of Chiapas, acting as her stand-in. His nephew, Larry William, helped me understand the pernicious nonsense of Ivy League college degrees. His kids, Breta, Lizzie, Paul and Geoffrey, allowed me to see what it could mean to have a sister or brother in lean times as well as fat. His sons-in-law Stephen, the young Colanero, and Richard, the young Cable, opened my eyes to how gracefully families can merge. His grandchildren Geoffrey, Courtenay, Shannon, Kathryn, Audrey, Mia, Heather, John, and Jessie, showed me the rich meaning behind the bittersweet glory of passing the torch.

After all the years, now well into old age, I'm still inspired by how Ronald keeps growing and changing; his love for and loyalty to Shanghai's courageous Ping Li, and her intrepid daughter, Ker Xin, give me hope for the human race.

O Plymouth! O Canada! O Uniontown! Protect the Hitchons; protect your son Ronald; protect my precious friend; protect his ghosts. Protect our families, one and all.

Prologue: Against School

I TAUGHT FOR THIRTY YEARS in some of the worst schools in Manhattan, and in some of the best, and during that time I became an expert in boredom. Boredom was everywhere in my world, and if you asked the kids, as I often did, *why* they felt so bored, they always gave me the same answers: They said the work was stupid, that it made no sense, that they already knew it. They said they wanted to be doing something real, not just sitting around. They said teachers didn't seem to know much about their subjects and clearly weren't interested in learning more. And the kids were right: their teachers were every bit as bored as they were.

Boredom is the common condition of schoolteachers, and anyone who has spent time in a teachers' lounge can vouch for the low energy, the whining, the dispirited attitudes, to be found there. When asked *why* they feel bored, teachers tend to blame kids, as you might expect. Who wouldn't get bored teaching students who are rude and interested only in grades? If even that. Of course, teachers are themselves products of the same twelve-year compulsory school programs that so thoroughly bore their students, and as school personnel they are trapped inside structures even more rigid than those imposed upon the children. Who, then, is to blame?

We all are. My grandfather taught me that. One afternoon when I was seven I complained to him of boredom, and he batted me hard on the head. He told me that I was never to use that term in his presence again, that if I was bored it was my fault and no one else's. The obligation to amuse and instruct myself was entirely my own, and people who didn't know that were childish people, to be avoided if possible. Certainly not to be trusted. That episode cured me of boredom forever, and here and there over the years I was able to pass on the lesson to some remarkable students. For the most part, however, I found it futile to challenge the official notion that boredom and childishness were the natural state of affairs in the classroom. Often I had to defy custom, and even bend the law, to help kids break out of this trap.

The empire struck back, of course; childish adults regularly conflate opposition with disloyalty. I once returned from a medical leave to discover all evidence of my having been granted leave had been deliberately destroyed, that my job had been terminated and I no longer possessed even a teaching license. After nine months of tormented effort I was able to retrieve the license when a school secretary testified to witnessing the plot unfold. In the meantime my family suffered more than I care to remember. By the time I finally retired in 1991, I had more than enough reason to think of our schools — with their long-term, cell-block-style forced confinement of both students and teachers — as virtual factories of childishness. Yet I honestly could not see *why* they had to be that way. My own experience revealed to me what many other teachers must learn along the way, too, yet keep to themselves for fear of reprisal: if we wanted we could easily and inexpensively jettison the old, stupid structures and help kids *take* an education rather than merely *receive* schooling. We could encourage the best qualities of youthfulness — curiosity, adventure, resilience, the capacity for surprising insight — simply by being more flexible about time, texts, and tests, by introducing kids to truly competent adults, and by giving each student the autonomy he or she needs in order to take a risk every now and then.

But we don't do that. And the more I asked why not, and persisted in thinking about the "problem" of schooling as an engineer might, the more I missed the point: What if there is no "problem" with our schools? What if they are the way they are, so expensively flying in the face of common sense and long experience in how children learn things, not because they are doing something wrong, but because they are doing something right? Is it possible that George W. Bush accidentally spoke the truth when he said he would "leave no child behind"? Could it be that our schools are designed to make sure not one of them ever really grows up?

Do we really need school? I don't mean education, just forced schooling: six classes a day, five days a week, nine months a year, for twelve years. Is this deadly routine really necessary? And if so, for what? Don't hide behind reading, writing, and arithmetic as a rationale, because 2 million happy homeschoolers have surely put that banal justification to rest. Even if they hadn't, a considerable number of well-known Americans never went through the twelve-year wringer our kids currently go through, and they turned out all right. George Washington, Benjamin Franklin, Thomas Jefferson, Abraham Lincoln? Someone taught them, to be sure, but they were not products of a school *system*, and not one of them was ever "graduated" from a secondary school. Throughout most of American history, kids generally didn't go to high school, yet the unschooled rose to be admirals, like Farragut; inventors, like Edison; captains of industry, like Carnegie and Rockefeller; writers, like Melville and Twain and Conrad; and even scholars, like Margaret Mead. In fact, until pretty recently people who reached the age of thirteen weren't looked upon as children at all. Ariel Durant, who co-wrote an enormous, and very good, multivolume history of the world with her husband Will, was happily married at fifteen, and who could reasonably claim Ariel Durant was an uneducated person? Unschooled, perhaps, but not uneducated.

We have been taught (that is, schooled) in this country to think "success" is synonymous with, or at least dependent upon, "schooling," but historically that isn't true in either an intellectual or a financial sense. And plenty of people throughout the world today find ways to educate themselves without resorting to a system of compulsory secondary schools that all too often resemble prisons. Why, then, do Americans confuse education with just such a system? What exactly is the purpose of our public schools?

Mass schooling of a compulsory nature really got its teeth into the United States between 1905 and 1915, though it was conceived of much earlier and pushed for throughout most of the nineteenth century. The reason given for this enormous upheaval of family life and cultural traditions was, roughly speaking, threefold:

1. To make good people.
2. To make good citizens.
3. To make each person his or her personal best.

These goals are still trotted out on a regular basis, and most of us accept them in one form or another as a decent definition of public education's mission, however short schools actually fall in achieving them. But we are dead wrong. Compounding our error is the fact that the national literature holds numerous and surprisingly consistent statements of compulsory schooling's true purpose. We have, for example, H.L. Mencken, who wrote in *The American Mercury* for April 1924 that the aim of public education is not

> ...to fill the young of the species with knowledge and awaken their intelligence.... Nothing could be further from the truth. The aim...is simply to reduce as many individuals as possible to the same safe level, to breed and train a standardized citizenry, to put down dissent and originality. That is its aim in the United States...and that is its aim everywhere else.

Because of Mencken's reputation as a satirist, you might be tempted to dismiss this passage as hyperbolic sarcasm. His article, however, goes on to trace the template for our own educational system back to the now vanished, though never to be forgotten, military state of Prussia. And although he was certainly aware of the irony that the US had recently been at war with Germany, the heir to Prussian thought and culture,

Mencken was being perfectly serious here. Our educational system really is Prussian in origin, and that really is cause for concern.

The odd fact of a Prussian provenance for our schools pops up again and again once you know to look for it. William James alluded to it many times at the turn of the twentieth century. Orestes Brownson, the hero of Christopher Lasch's 1991 book, *The True and Only Heaven,* was publicly denouncing the deliberate Prussianization of American schools back in the 1840s. Horace Mann's "Seventh Annual Report" to the Massachusetts Board of Education in 1843 is essentially a paean to the land of Frederick the Great and a call for its schooling to be brought here. That Prussian culture loomed large in America is hardly surprising, given our early association with that utopian state. A Prussian served as Washington's aide during the Revolutionary War, and so many German-speaking people had settled here by 1795 that Congress considered publishing a German-language edition of the federal laws. But what shocks is that we should so eagerly have adopted one of the very worst aspects of Prussian culture: an educational system deliberately designed to produce mediocre intellects, to hamstring the inner life, to deny students appreciable leadership skills, and to ensure docile and incomplete citizens — all in order to render the populace "manageable."

It was from James Bryant Conant — president of Harvard for twenty years, WWI poison-gas specialist, WWII executive of the atomic-bomb project, high commissioner of the American zone in Germany after WWII, and truly one of the most influential figures of the twentieth century — that I first got wind of the real purposes of American schooling. Without Conant, we would probably not have the same style and degree of standardized testing that we enjoy today, nor would we be blessed with gargantuan high schools that warehouse 2,000 to 4,000 students at a time, like the famous Columbine High School in Littleton, Colorado. Shortly after I retired from teaching I picked up Conant's 1959 book-length essay, *The Child, the Parent*

and the State, and was more than a little intrigued to see him mention in passing that the modern schools we attend were the result of a "revolution" engineered between 1905 and 1930. A revolution? He declines to elaborate, but he does direct the curious and the uninformed to Alexander Inglis's 1918 book, *Principles of Secondary Education*, in which "one saw this revolution through the eyes of a revolutionary."

Inglis, for whom an honor lecture in education at Harvard is named, makes it perfectly clear that compulsory schooling on this continent was intended to be just what it had been for Prussia in the 1820s: a fifth column into the burgeoning democratic movement that threatened to give peasants and proletarians a voice at the bargaining table. Modern, industrialized, compulsory schooling was to make a sort of surgical intervention into the prospective unity of these underclasses. Divide children by subject, by age-grading, by constant rankings on tests, and by many other more subtle means, and it was unlikely that the ignorant mass of mankind, separated in childhood, would ever re-integrate into a dangerous whole.

Inglis breaks down the purpose — the *actual* purpose — of modern schooling into six basic functions, any one of which is enough to curl the hair of those innocent enough to believe the three traditional goals of education listed earlier:

1. The *adjustive* or *adaptive* function. Schools are to establish fixed habits of reaction to authority. This, of course, precludes critical judgment completely. It also pretty much destroys the idea that useful or interesting material should be taught, because you can't test for *reflexive* obedience until you know whether you can make kids learn, and do, foolish and boring things.
2. The *integrating* function. This might well be called "the conformity function," because its intention is to make children as alike as possible. People who conform are predictable, and this is of great use to those who wish to harness and manipulate a large labor force.

3. The *diagnostic and directive* function. School is meant to determine each student's proper social role. This is done by logging evidence mathematically and anecdotally on cumulative records. As in "your permanent record." Yes, you do have one.
4. The *differentiating* function. Once their social role has been "diagnosed," children are to be sorted by role and trained only so far as their destination in the social machine merits — and not one step further. So much for making kids their personal best.
5. The *selective* function. This refers not to human choice at all but to Darwin's theory of natural selection as applied to what he called "the favored races." In short, the idea is to help things along by consciously attempting to improve the breeding stock. Schools are meant to tag the unfit — with poor grades, remedial placement, and other punishments — clearly enough that their peers will accept them as inferior and effectively bar them from the reproductive sweepstakes. That's what all those little humiliations from first grade onward were intended to do: wash the dirt down the drain.
6. The *propaedeutic* function. The societal system implied by these rules will require an elite group of caretakers. To that end, a small fraction of the kids will quietly be taught how to manage this continuing project, how to watch over and control a population deliberately dumbed down and declawed in order that government might proceed unchallenged and corporations might never want for obedient labor.

Those, unfortunately, are the purpose of mandatory public education in this country. And lest you consider Inglis an isolated crank with a rather too cynical take on the educational enterprise, you should know he was hardly alone in championing these ideas. Conant himself, building on the ideas of Horace Mann and others, campaigned tirelessly for an American school system designed along the same lines. Men like George Peabody, who funded the cause of mandatory schooling throughout the South, surely understood that the Prussian system was useful in creating not only a harmless electorate and a servile labor force but also a virtual herd of mindless consumers. In time a great number of industrial titans came to recognize the enormous profits to be had by cultivating and tending just such a herd via public education, among them Andrew Carnegie and John D. Rockefeller.

There you have it. Now you know. We don't need Karl Marx's conception of a grand warfare between the classes to see that it is in the interest of complex management, economic or political, to dumb people down, to demoralize them, to divide them from one another, and to discard them if they don't conform. Class may frame the proposition, as when Woodrow Wilson, then president of Princeton University, said the following to the New York City School Teachers Association in 1909: "We want one class of persons to have a liberal education, and we want another class of persons, a very much larger class, of necessity, in every society, to forgo the privileges of a liberal education and fit themselves to perform specific difficult manual tasks." But the motives behind the disgusting decisions that bring about these ends need not be class-based at all. They can stem purely from fear, or from the by-now-familiar belief that "efficiency" is the paramount virtue, rather than love, liberty, laughter or hope. Above all, they can stem from simple greed.

There were vast fortunes to be made, after all, in an economy based on mass production and organized to favor the large corporation rather than the small business or the family farm. But mass production required mass consumption, and at the turn of the twentieth century most Americans considered it both unnatural and unwise to buy things they didn't actually need. Mandatory schooling was a godsend on that count. School didn't have to train kids in any direct sense to think they should consume nonstop, because it did something even better: it encouraged them not to think at all. And that left them sitting ducks for another great invention of the modern era — marketing.

Now, you needn't have studied marketing to know that there are two groups of people who can always be convinced to consume more than they need to: addicts and children. School has done a pretty good job of turning our children into addicts, but a spectacular job of turning our children into children. Again, this is no accident. Theorists from Plato to Rousseau to our own Dr. Inglis knew that if children could be cloistered with other children, stripped of responsibility and independence, encouraged to develop only the trivializing emotions of greed, envy, jealousy, and fear, they would grow older but never truly grow up. In the 1934 edition of his once well-known book *Public Education in the United States,* Ellwood P. Cubberley detailed and praised the way the strategy of successive school enlargements had extended childhood by two to six years already, and forced schooling was at that point still quite new. This same Cubberley was an intimate colleague of Dr. Inglis: both were in charge of textbook publishing divisions at Houghton Mifflin — Cubberley as chief of elementary school texts; Inglis of secondary school texts. Cubberley was dean of Stanford's influential School of Education as well, a friendly correspondent of Conant at Harvard. He had written in his book *Public School Administration* (1922) that "our schools are... factories in which the raw products (children) are to be shaped and fashioned.... And that it is the business of the school to build its pupils according to the specifications laid down."

It's perfectly obvious from our society today what those specifications were. Maturity has by now been banished from nearly every aspect of our lives. Easy divorce laws have removed the need to work at relationships; easy credit has removed the need for fiscal self-control; easy entertainment has removed the need to learn to entertain oneself; easy answers have removed the need to ask questions. We have become a nation of children, happy to surrender our judgments and our wills to political exhortations and commercial blandishments that would insult actual adults. We buy televisions, and then we buy the things we see on the television. We buy $150 sneakers whether we need them or not, and when they fall apart too soon we buy another pair. We drive SUVs and believe the lie that they constitute a kind of life insurance, even when we're upside-down in them. And, worst of all, we don't bat an eye when Ari Fleischer* tells us to "be careful what you say," even if we remember having been told somewhere back in school that America is the land of the free. We simply buy that one, too. Our schooling, as intended, has seen to it.

~

Now for the good news. Once you understand the logic behind modern schooling, its tricks and traps are fairly easy to avoid. School trains children to be employees and consumers; teach your own to be leaders and adventurers. School trains children to obey reflexively; teach your own to think critically and independently. Well-schooled kids have a low threshold for boredom; help your own to develop an inner life so that they'll never be bored. Urge them to take on the serious material, the *grown-up* material, in history, literature, philosophy, music, art, economics, theology — all the stuff schoolteachers know well enough to avoid. Challenge your kids with plenty of solitude so that they can learn to enjoy their own company, to conduct inner dialogues. Well-schooled people are conditioned to dread being alone; they seek constant companionship through the TV, the computer, the cell phone, and through shallow friendships quickly acquired, quickly abandoned. Your children should have a more important life, and they can.

First, though, wake up to what our schools really are: laboratories of experimentation on young minds, drill centers for the habits and attitudes that corporate society demands. Mandatory education serves children only incidentally; its real purpose is to turn them into servants. Don't let your own have their childhoods extended, not even for a day. If David Farragut could take command of a captured British warship as a preteen, if Ben Franklin could apprentice himself to a printer at the same age (then put himself through a course of study that would choke a Yale senior today), there's no telling what your own kids could do. After a long life, and thirty years in the public

* Ari Fleischer was a Press Secretary under President George W. Bush.

school trenches, I've concluded that genius is as common as dirt. We suppress genius because we haven't yet figured out how to manage a population of educated men and women. The solution, I think, is simple and glorious. Let them manage themselves.

"Against School" was first published as the cover essay in Harper's *magazine.*

The actual corridor where the author spent much of his adult life

1

Everything You Know about Schools is Wrong

> In 1909 a factory inspector did an informal survey of 500 working children in 20 factories. She found that 412 of them would rather work in the terrible conditions of the factories than return to school.
>
> — Helen Todd, "Why Children Work"
> *McClure's Magazine*, April 1913

Running the World

In 1919, in the heady aftermath of World War victory parades and an intoxicating sense that nothing was forbidden to the United States, including the very alteration of human nature, Professor Arthur Calhoun's *Social History of the Family* notified the academic world that something profound was going on behind the scenes in the nation's schools. Big changes were being made to the idea of family. And it was a consummation to be celebrated by Calhoun's crowd, although not by everyone.

Calhoun wrote that the fondest wish of utopian thinkers was coming true: children were passing from blood families "into the custody of community experts." In time, he wrote, the dream of Darwin and Galton would become reality through the agency of public education, "designed to check the mating of the unfit." The dream of scientific population control.

Not everyone was as impressed as Calhoun with the school agenda discreetly being inserted into classrooms beyond public oversight. Mayor John Hylan of New York City made an elliptical remark in a public address back in 1922 which preserves some of the weirdness of that moment. Hylan announced that the schools of the city had been seized by "tentacles" of "an invisible government, just as an octopus would seize prey," a pointed echo of the chilling pronouncement made years earlier by British prime minister Benjamin Disraeli, when he claimed that all important events were controlled by an invisible government, of which the public was unaware. The particular octopus Hylan meant was the Rockefeller Foundation.

The 1920s were a boom period in compulsory schooling, as well as the stock market. By 1928 the book *A Sociological Philosophy of Education* was claiming, "It is the business of teachers to run not merely schools but the world." A year later, Edward Thorndike of Rockefeller-sponsored Columbia Teachers College, creator of a curious new academic specialty called "Educational Psychology," went on record with this dramatic announcement: "Academic subjects are of little value." His colleague at Teachers College, William Kirkpatrick, declared in his own book, *Education and the Social Crisis,* that "the whole game of rearing the young was being taken over by experts." It seemed only common sense to Dr. Kilpatrick. Family, after all, was a retrograde institution, why should mom and dad know better than experts how to bring up baby?

The Control of Human Behavior

On April 11, 1933, the president of the Rockefeller Foundation, Max Mason, announced a comprehensive national program underway, with the help of the Foundation, to allow "the control of human behavior." School figured centrally in its design. Max Muller, an Eastern European geneticist, inspired Rockefeller to invest heavily in control of human evolution. Muller was using X-rays to override normal genetic laws, including mutations in fruit flies. Mutation appeared to open the door to the scientific control of all life.

In Muller's mind, as to Galton and Darwin before him, planned breeding of human beings was the key to paradise. His thinking was enthusiastically endorsed by great scientists and by powerful economic interests alike. Muller won the Nobel Prize and reduced his scheme to a 1,500-word *Geneticists' Manifesto*, signed by 22 distinguished American and British biologists. State action should separate worthwhile breeding stock from the great mass of evolutionary dead-end material. The *Manifesto* can still be Googled. What had been discussed behind closed doors in the 1870s, before we had forced schooling, had broken through into public discourse, at least in high-policy circles, and in the writings of sophisticated literary artists like F. Scott Fitzgerald. A movement away from democratic egalitarian ideals was underway, which Fitzgerald alludes to in *The Great Gatsby*.

In simple language, on the most basic level of institutional management, smart kids had to be kept from stupid ones; Horace Mann's common school notion that all levels of society would mix together in the classroom to create social harmony was now officially stone dead, except for rhetorical purposes. A few months before the *Manifesto* began circulating aggressively, an executive director of the National Education Association announced the NEA expected "to accomplish by education what dictators in Europe are seeking to do by compulsion and force." That's straightforward enough, isn't it?

World War II drove the eugenic project underground, but hardly slowed its advance. Following the end of hostilities, school became an open battleground between old-fashioned, modest, reading, writing and arithmetic ambitions of historic schooling, and proponents of advanced academic thinking, located mainly in project offices of great corporate non-profit foundations like Carnegie and Rockefeller — men who worked diligently to lead institutional schooling toward a scientific rationalization of all social affairs. Two congressional investigations, one in 1915 and one in 1959, came to the identical conclusion that school policy in the new pedagogical order was being deliberately created far from public oversight, in corporate offices — inserted into the school mechanism by a sophisticated, highly nuanced campaign of influence, invisible to public awareness. Neither report received much public attention. While both are available for examination today, virtually nobody is aware they even exist. Every major teachers' college in America flushed them down the memory hole, under whose orders nobody knows.

Two decades after WWII, between 1967 and 1974, teacher training was radically revamped through the coordinated efforts of important private foundations, select universities, think-tanks, and government agencies, encouraged by major global corporations and harmonized through the US Office of Education and a few key state education departments, particularly those of California, Texas, New York, Michigan, Indiana, Florida, and Pennsylvania.

Three milestones in this transformation were: (1) an extensive government exercise in futurology called *Designing Education for the Future;* (2) *The Behavioral Science Teacher Education Project;* and (3) Benjamin Bloom's multi-volume *Taxonomy of Educational Objectives,* an enormous manual of over 1,000 pages out of Bloom's office at the University of Chicago. Later, this work impacted every school in America. Bloom's massive effort is the work of a genuine academic madman, constituting, in his own words, "a tool to classify the ways individuals are to act, think and feel as the result of some unit of instruction." It's the "think and feel" part that gives the game away. Simple fascism would have stopped at *action,* but as Orwell warned in *1984,* something deeper than fascism was happening.

Drawing on the new technology of "behavioral psychology," children would be forced to learn "proper" thoughts, feelings, and actions, while "improper" attitudes brought from home were "remediated." Seething and bubbling in the darkness outside the innocent cluster of little red schoolhouses coast to coast a chemical wedding was being brewed worthy of Doctor Frankenstein. On all levels of schooling, experiments were authorized upon children without any public notice. Think of it as the Tuskegee Syphillis Experiment writ large. Testing was an essential part of the experiment — to locate each child's *mental susceptibility* on an official rating scale.

Bloom's insane epic is reminiscent of *The Complete System of Medical Policing*, proposed for Prussia by another mad German doctor in the late 18th century (in which every citizen was charged with continually spying on every other citizen, detecting any sign of disease pathology, even a sniffle, and reporting it at once to authorities for remedial action), Bloom spawned a horde of descendant forms: mastery learning; outcomes-based education; school-to-work; classroom/business "partnerships;" and more. You can detect Bloom at work in any initiative which seeks to classify students for the convenience of social managers and businesses. Bloom-inspired programs are constructed so as to offer useful data for controlling the minds and movements of the young — mapping the next adult generation for various agencies of social engineering.

The second pillar of change agentry, *Designing Education for the Future*, belies its benign title and would well repay a disciplined read-through of its semi-literate prose. Produced by the US Office of Education, it redefined "education" after the Prussian fashion as "a means to achieve important economic and social goals of a national character." No mention of personal goals are in evidence. State education agencies were henceforth ordered to act as on-site federal enforcers, ensuring compliance of local schools to central directives. Each state education department was to become "an agent of change," and these were advised to give up "independent identity as well as authority," accepting a junior partnership with the federal government. Or suffer financial penalties for disobedience.

Finally, consider the third gigantic project, twice the size of Bloom's *Taxonomy*: the *Behavioral Science Teacher Education Project* (contract number: OEC-0-9-320424-4042), BSTEP for short, which clearly sets down government policy intentions for compulsory schooling, outlining reforms to be *forced* on the US after 1967. Institutional schooling, we learn, will be required to "impersonally manipulate" the future of an America in which "each individual will receive at birth a multi-purpose identification number." This will enable employers "and other controllers" to keep track of the common mass and to expose it to "direct or subliminal influence when necessary." Readers of the BSTEP document, which entered public consciousness (to the minor extent it has) only when a former Department of Justice employee blew the whistle, were invited to consider a future America in which "few will be able to maintain control over their own opinions."

BSTEP tells us that "chemical experimentation" on minors will become normal procedure after 1967, a pointed foreshadowing of Ritalin, Adderol, and other chemical "interventions" which accompany little Johnny to grade school these days. The document identifies the future as one in which a small elite will control all important matters, a world in which participatory democracy will disappear, reduced to a meaningless voting prerogative in electoral campaigns, campaigns in which all serious candidates have been pre-selected to exclude troublemakers. Politicians will still be able to *threaten* substantial change, but to deliver only token efforts to that end after election.

Postmodern schooling, BSTEP continues, will focus on "attitudes and skills compatible with a non-work world." Like "pleasure cultivation." You'll have no difficulty seeing the "socialized" classroom of WWI school reform — itself a radical departure from mental and character development — had evolved by 1967 into a full-scale laboratory of psychological manipulation.

How many schoolteachers were aware of what they actually were a part of? Surely a number close to zero. In schoolteaching, as in hamburger-flipping, the paycheck is the decisive ingredient. No insult is meant, at bottom this is what *realpolitik* means. We all have to eat.

Teachers as Therapists

The conversion of schools into laboratories was assisted by a curious phenomenon of the middle to late 1960s: a tremendous rise in school violence and general chaos which followed a now-forgotten policy declaration cooked up at the Ford Foundation, one which announced that henceforth, disciplining of children must reflect due process practices of the court system. Teachers and administrators were stripped overnight of any effective ability to keep order, since due process apparatus, of necessity slow and deliberate, is inadequate to the sudden outbreaks of childish mischief which occur, even in presumably good schools. A rough *ad hoc* justice is the principal way order was maintained historically. Without it, *le deluge!*

Denied access to the ancient catalogue of *ad hoc* disciplinary tactics, classrooms descended into chaos, disorder spiraled out of control — passing into dangerous terrain from what once had been only a realm of petty annoyance. As word passed through student ranks that teachers' hands were tied, crowds of excited kids surged through hallways, howling, screaming, banging on doors, attacking one another. Even displays of public fornication weren't unknown — at least not at my own school assignment at Intermediate School 44 in Community School District 3 on the Upper Westside of Manhattan, smack in the middle of one of the wealthiest communities in the country. But appeals to authority for help went unanswered.

Instead of interrupting the fornicators, arsonists, muggers, and other hooligans forcibly (which we were repeatedly warned would expose teachers to legal action), the new policy required teachers to file complaints (on official complaint forms *only*). After that, a hearing date would be set and, assuming the accused showed up, both sides had the right to be represented by counsel, to summon witnesses, to cross-examine. When that drama was complete, a ruling would issue from the assigned referee. Not at once, but in due time. If "convicted," students had the right to appeal the decision, and the whole wheel would turn once again. This in a universe of 1,200 12-to-14- year-old kids.

Now imagine serious or semi-serious incidents each and every day, a hundred a week, four thousand a year, each necessitating forms, testimony, adjudication, punishment (or not), appeals... The Behavioral Science Teacher Education Project, occurring at the peak of this violent period, demanded teacher training institutes prepare all graduates to be teacher-therapists, translating prescriptions of social psychology into "practical action" in the classroom. Curriculum had been redefined. Now teaching followed suit.

We Don't Need Brains

Between 1896 and 1920, a small group of industrialists and financiers, together with their private charitable foundations, heavily subsidized university chairs, researchers, and school administrators, actually spent more money on forced schooling's early years than did the government. Just two men, Carnegie and Rockefeller, were themselves spending more as late as 1915. In this *laissez-faire* fashion a system of "modern" schooling was constructed without any public participation, or even much public knowledge. Motives were complex, but it will clear your head wonderfully to listen to what Rockefeller's General Education Board thought the mission should be. Its statement occurs in multiple forms, this one taken from a 1906 document called *Occasional Letter Number One:*

> In our dreams...people yield themselves with perfect docility to our molding hands. The present educational conventions [of intellectual and moral education] fade from our minds, and unhampered by tradition we work our own good will upon a grateful and responsive folk. We shall not try to make these people or any of their children into philosophers or men of learning or men of science. We have not to raise up from among them authors, educators, poets, or men of letters. We shall not search for embryo great artists, painters, musicians, nor lawyers, doctors, preachers, politicians, statesmen — of whom we have an ample supply. The task we set before ourselves is very simple...we will organize children...and teach them to do in a perfect way the things their fathers and mothers are doing in an imperfect way.

In other words, they didn't want brains or talent, just obedience. Who is the "we" here? This mission statement of the General Education

Board should be read more than once, until the illusions about school so carefully implanted in your mind are broken.

"Is This Nuts?"

At the start of WWII, millions of men showed up at registration offices to take low-level academic tests before being inducted. Years of maximum mobilization were 1942 through 1944, and our fighting force had mostly been schooled in the 1930s. Eighteen million were tested and 17,280,000 were judged to have the minimum competence in reading necessary to be a soldier — a 96 percent literacy rate.

This was a two percent fall-off from the 98 percent of ten years earlier, but the dip was too small to worry anyone. The generals might have been more concerned had they been able to foresee profound changes being foreshadowed by this nearly imperceptible two percent decline.

~

WWII was over in 1945. Six years later, another war began in Korea and several million more men were tested for military service. This time, 600,000 were rejected. Literacy in the draft pool had mysteriously dropped to 81 percent from 96 percent, even though all that was needed to classify a soldier as literate was fourth-grade reading proficiency. In a few short years from WWII to Korea, a terrifying problem of adult illiteracy had appeared, seemingly from nowhere.

The Korean War group had received most of *its* schooling in the 1940s while the conflict with Germany and Japan was being waged. It had more years in school, with more professionally trained teachers in attendance, and more scientifically selected textbooks than the WWII men. Yet, it could not read, write, count, speak, or think as well as the earlier, less-schooled contingent.

A new American war began in Vietnam in the middle 1960s. By its end in 1973, the number of men found non-inductible by reason of inability to read safety instructions, interpret road signs, decipher orders — the number found illiterate in other words — had reached 27 percent of the total pool. Vietnam-era young men had been schooled in the 1950s and 1960s, *far more intensely schooled than either of the two earlier groups*, but now the four percent illiteracy of 1941, transmuted into the 19 percent illiteracy rate of 1952, was 27 percent.

And not only had the fraction of barely competent and competent readers dropped to 73 percent, but even a substantial chunk of these struggled mightily, unable to read a newspaper (or anything else) for pleasure. They could not sustain a thought or an argument, could not write well enough to manage their own affairs without assistance.

Mute evidence of rising ineptitude is more compelling when tracked through the very minimal requirements of Army enlistment tests, because SAT scores are frequently "renormed" (inflated), whether to conceal the decline or not, your guess is as good as mine.

By 1940, literacy as a national number stood at 96 percent for whites, 80 percent for blacks. Four of five blacks were literate in spite of all disadvantages. Yet, six decades later, the Adult Literacy Survey and the National Assessment of Educational Progress reported a 40 percent illiteracy rate among blacks — doubling the earlier deficiency — and a 17 percent rate for whites, more than quadrupling it. Yet money spent on schooling in real terms had grown 350 percent.

Charles Murray and Richard Hernnstein contended in a national #1 bestseller, *The Bell Curve*, that this was the result of selective breeding. Smart people got together with smart people — and dumb with dumb. If you're a eugenicist that sounds just right, until you remember the inconvenient military data. The terrifying drop in literacy between the end of WWII and the beginning of the Korean War happened *inside a single decade*. Even the most fervent natural selection enthusiast wouldn't argue things work that quickly.

The Bell Curve held that violence in black society was genetically programmed; but once again, data from outside the charmed circle in America pushing this biological reality was contradictory. My control group comes from South Africa, where 31 million blacks lived as of the year 2000 — the same number as in the US. During 1989 to 1991, civil war conditions existed in South Africa. Then how to account for the embarrassing truth that death by violence among blacks there was only *one-quarter of what it was in America?*

A second corrective piece of information turned up as I was writing this: data from nearly all-black Jamaica for the year 2004 shows the literacy rate there at 98.5 percent, considerably higher than the 2005 American rate for *whites* — 83 percent.

What might explain the sharp decline in literacy among blacks, if *not* bad biology? Consider this: during WWII, American public schools — first in urban areas, then everywhere — were converted from phonetic ways of instruction (the ancient "alphabet system") to non-phonetic methods which involved memorizing whole word units, and lots of guessing for unfamiliar words. Whites had been learning to read at home for 300 years the old-fashioned way — matching spoken sounds to written letters — and white homes preserved this tool even when schools left it behind. There was a resource available to whites which hardly existed for blacks. During slavery, blacks had been forbidden to learn to read; as late as 1930 they averaged only three to four years of schooling. When teachers stopped teaching a phonetic system — known to work — blacks had no fallback position.

By 1952 the Army had hired a brigade of psychologists to expose what it believed must be mass fraud, so many were failing to qualify. As Regna Lee Woods described it in Checker Finn and Diane Ravitch's *Network News and Reviews:*

> After the psychologists told the officers the graduates *weren't* faking, Defense Department administrators knew something terrible had happened to grade school reading instruction. Why they remained silent, no one knows. The switch to reading instruction that worked should have been made then. But it wasn't.

In 1995 a student-teacher of fifth graders in Minneapolis wrote a letter to the editor of the *Star-Tribune* complaining about radically dumbed-down curriculum. She wrote that 113 years earlier fifth graders in

Minneapolis were reading William Shakespeare, Henry Thoreau, George Washington, Sir Walter Scott, Mark Twain, Benjamin Franklin, Oliver Wendell Holmes, John Bunyan, Daniel Webster, Samuel Johnson, Lewis Caroll, Thomas Jefferson, Emerson, and others like them in the *Appleton School Reader*, but that today,

> I was told children are not to be expected to spell the following words correctly: back, big, call, came, can, day, did, dog, down, get, good, have, he, home, if, in, is, it, like, little, man, morning, mother, my, night, off, out, over, people, play, ran, said, saw, she, some, soon, their, them, there, time, two, too, up, us, very, water, we, went, where, when, will, would, etc. Is this nuts?

Transcending Nature

It's time to meet William Torrey Harris, US Commissioner of Education from 1889 to 1906, the premier Hegelian philosopher in America, editor of *The Journal of Speculative Philosophy*. Other than Ellwood P. Cubberley and James Bryant Conant, no professional pedagogue ever approached the influence Harris once wielded. Harris standardized our national schooling and Germanized it. Teacher colleges gloss over Harris, referring to him as a conservative defender of classical education standards, but he was intensely radical, regarding children as the absolute property of the political state, and he was a personal friend of Andrew Carnegie — the steel man who nourished a hope that all work could be yoked to cradle-to-grave schooling — the grandfather of all school-to-work projects.

Perhaps Walt Whitman had been anticipating Harris and Carnegie when he wrote that "only Hegel is fit for America." Hegel, the protean Prussian philosopher whose power molded Karl Marx on the one hand and J. P. Morgan on the other, the two men different faces of Hegel, as the Soviet Union and America danced also to the music of this Prussian. What Hegel taught that intrigued the powerful then and now was that history could be deliberately managed by skillfully provoking crises out of public view and then demanding national unity to meet those crises — a disciplined unity under cover of which leadership privileges approached the absolute.

Waiting for Teacher to Grant Your Turn

Harris and associates, known to academic philosophy as the "St. Louis Hegelians," worked toward a strange goal, bringing an end to history. Fixing global society into frozen relationships in which all argument would end, and with argument gone, the urge to war and revolution as well. Just amicable folk waiting around pleasantly for someone to tell them what to do, like the Eloi in H.G. Wells' *The Time Machine*. Waiting in tutelary relationships for someone to signal each individual's turn.

The tool to build such a society was psychological alienation, said Harris. To alienate children from themselves so they could no longer turn inward for strength, to alienate them from families, traditions, religions, cultures — so no outside source of advice could contradict the will of the political state. You need to hear Harris' own voice now, to fully appreciate what the principal school figure in America was thinking at the very moment institutional schooling was coming together here:

> Ninety-nine [students] out of a hundred are automata, careful to walk in prescribed paths, careful to follow the prescribed custom. This is not an accident but the result of substantial education which, scientifically defined, is the subsumption of the individual....
>
> The great purpose of school [self-alienation] can be realized better in dark, airless, ugly places.... It is to master the physical self, to transcend the beauty of nature. School should develop the power to withdraw from the external world. [*The Philosophy of Education*, 1906]

There's a commonsensical lunacy here, a rich manure of pragmatism inherent in this which deserves being held up to the light.

Self-alienation as a secret success formula for a mass production industrial/commercial economy (and the class-driven social order which complements it) isn't as wrong as first impressions make it sound. Consider that such a social order can't produce very much satisfying work — the kind where personal sovereignty is exercised. As this social order matures, so many dissatisfied people are its byproduct that daily life is rocked by instability. But if you can be persuaded to blame yourself rather than a group of villains for your miserable lot, the dangerous gas goes out of the social balloon.

When you flip hamburgers, sit at a computer all day, unpack and shelve merchandise from China year after year, you manage the tedium better if you have a shallow inner life, one you can escape through booze, drugs, sex, media, or other low level addictive behaviors. Easier to keep sane if your inner life is shallow. School, thought Harris the great American schoolman, should prepare ordinary men and women for lifetimes of alienation. Can you say he wasn't fully rational?

The transformation of school from a place of modest ambitions centering around reading, writing, arithmetic, and decency into a behavioral training laboratory ordered up by "certain industrialists and the innovative who were altering the nature of the industrial process" (as Harvard president James Bryant Conant wrote), has acted to poison the American experiment. After 30 years in a public school classroom serving this creature, when I quit teaching in 1991 I promised myself I would bear witness to what I had seen and, forgive me, done. This book is my way of keeping that promise.

The Crisis of Democracy

Toward the end of the nineteenth century, far-sighted American businessmen, having metaphorically conquered the world, set about bringing the ancient dream of utopia alive through a psychological strategy pioneered in Germany. They would colonize the minds of the young, wipe the messy slates clean so they could be written upon fresh. What religion had conceived and philosophy affirmed now took on new urgency as science spelled out the biological disaster which might attend any delay. Darwin himself had spoken. And the laboratories of Germany.

Horace Mann's efforts to make school attendance compulsory were bankrolled by men of wealth, including the brilliant Peabody family of New England. Mann was promised Daniel Webster's seat in Congress if he could pull off the trick, and he did, winning the Congressional seat as a prize. But we know the America of Mann's day was already formidably literate and full of opportunity, so any attempt to portray this as philanthropy shouldn't be taken seriously.

In every age, men of wealth and power have approached education for ordinary people with suspicion because it is certain to stimulate discontent, certain to awaken desires impossible to gratify. In April 1872, the US Bureau of Education's *Circular of Information* left nothing to the imagination when it discussed something it called "the problem of educational schooling." According to the Bureau, by inculcating accurate knowledge workers would "perceive and calculate their grievances," making them "redoubtable foes" in labor struggles! Best not have *that*.

Thirteen years later in 1885, the Senate Committee on Education and Labor issued a report which contains this forceful observation on page 1382: "We believe that education is one of the principal causes of discontent of late years manifesting itself among the laboring classes." Teaching the means to become broadly knowledgeable, deeply analytical, and effectively expressive has disturbed policy thinkers since Solomon, because these skills introduce danger into the eternal need of leaders to manage crowds in the interests of the best people.

Adam Smith's *Wealth of Nations* called for "educational schooling" to correct the human damage caused by mindless working environments, but Andrew Carnegie, writing 126 years after Smith, in *The Empire of Business* disagreed. Educational schooling, said Carnegie, gives working people bad attitudes, it teaches what is useless, it imbues the future workforce with "false ideas" that give it "a distaste for practical life."

In 1949 in an essay which has slipped through the cracks of history, *Science and the Moral Life*, the academic, Max Otto, found the heavy involvement of business behind the curtain of schooling far from odd. He said it was something naturally to be expected. A stupendous revolution in marketing had taken place under the public nose, one brought about by the reality of mass production which could not be constrained to simply *meet* human demands, but instead imposed the demands of production on human wishes. Where once the conventional laws of supply and demand put the buyer in the driver's seat, in the topsy-turvy world of financial capitalism *demand had to be created* for whatever could be supplied most profitably at the moment. To keep this golden goose laying eggs, consumption had to be taught as the most important end of life. It was this new reality, he said, that explained business manipulation of schooling:

> It is natural businessmen should seek to influence the enactment and administration of laws, national and international, and that they should try to control education.

Keep that uppermost in your mind as you read my book.

A Different Agenda

The new forced schooling octopus taught anyone unable to escape its tentacles that inert knowledge — memorizing the dots — is the gold standard of intellectual achievement. Not connecting those dots. It set out to create a reflexive obedience to official directions as opposed to accepting responsibility for one's own learning.

These habit trainings are among the most important weapons of mass instruction. On the higher levels of the school pyramid, among those labeled "gifted" and "talented," the standard is more sophisticated: there children are required to memorize both dots as well as what experts say is the correct way to connect those dots into narratives: even to memorize several conflicting expert analyses in a simulation of genuine critical thinking. Original thinking in dot connection is patronized at times, but always subtly discouraged. Twelve to twenty years of stupefying memorization drills weakens the hardiest intellects.

Long before this habit training took hold, America was, by any historical yardstick, formidably well-educated, a place of aggressively free speech and argument — dynamically entrepreneurial, dazzlingly inventive, and as egalitarian a place as human nature could tolerate. Social class distinctions were relatively fluid since merit in simple free-market economies produces its own rewards, including advantageous marriages. Although the same currents of class privilege which ran in Europe were always present in America, the crucial difference was they were vigorously contested there.

America was literate beyond anybody's wildest dreams, and not merely book-literate. Americans were broadly proficient in the formidable "active literacies" of writing, argumentation, and public speaking; things which had actually been a crime to teach ordinary people under British colonial rule. Foreign travelers like Tocqueville were surprised and impressed with what the new nation demonstrated in action about the talents of ordinary men and women — abilities customarily suppressed in Europe among the common classes.

We were embarked on a unique libertarian path right up to the Civil War, until post-war fallout put an end to its career in reality, although the original myths are still with us. The transition from an entrepreneurial economy to a mass production economy, which began soon after the end of hostilities, wrenched the country from its freedom-loving course and placed it along the path toward industrial capitalism — with its need for visible underclasses and a large, rootless proletariat to make it work.

But the record of our libertarian beginnings is so striking it cannot be erased from the historical record. It persisted long enough to provide a wealth of practical evidence that successful alternative formats exist through which young people can win through to effective minds and characters. Alternative, that is, to confinement with hired mercenaries which, harsh as it sounds, is the current system.

Ben Franklin, son of a candlemaker in a family of seventeen, was the perfect emblem of the difference. Make his short autobiography a must-read, to be read closely more than once. Franklin was the product of brilliant and daring curriculum design with the designer Franklin himself. He was an open-source learner for the ages and he will generously show you how the trick is done.

The Myth of a Golden Age

Long before we actually converted schools to the Prussian model beginning in 1852, the matter had been carefully discussed in drawing rooms, and in the backrooms of business and politics. As early as 1840 in New England, a prominent public intellectual named Orestes Brownson began to publicly denounce in speeches and writings what he called a monumental conspiracy on the part of important men to subvert the Constitution, using northern Germany's rigid institution of forced schooling as its principal weapon. You can read about Brownson and those critical days of school history in Christopher Lasch's *True and Only Heaven.*

By the end of the same decade, Mann's (imaginary[1]) visit to see Prussian schools in action — and his famously favorable report of that visit to the Boston School Committee — soon led to the first successful[2] school law in US history. Brownson's larger theory, that a group existed out of sight intent on recasting American national life to meet British and German standards, should be kept in mind as we proceed into the dark world of compulsory schooling.

Right from its advent the school institution was not popular. There wasn't any rush to sign on. It took a full 15 years for one more state to come aboard, but a telling clue exists to let us know where the evangelical energy driving the scheme was actually being housed. Although no second American *state* followed Massachusetts for a decade and a half, the tiny District of Columbia adopted compulsion in

[1] Mann, through careless planning, actually arrived in Prussia after schools were closed for the summer, a fact he concealed from the committee.

[2] Earlier school laws existed, but they were widely ignored.

its schools almost at once! It was from Washington's bribes, subsidies, and cajolings that institutional schooling spread, not from the merit of the idea.

The myth of a golden age of public schooling is the creation of Ellwood P. Cubberley, Dean of Teacher Education at Stanford University. There never was such a thing. Cubberley rose to become a leader of the school group around WWI, and remained a close associate of all other names of consequence in the founding period. He acted, *de facto*, as a beloved historian of American schooling until the 1960s.

Eliminating Local Voices

At the start of the compulsion era there were approximately 135,000 separate citizen school boards, perhaps more, each with seven to nine very solid and very local men and women as board members, watchdogs over the local institution. Messy as their operation was — and you can get a sample of how they worked by reading Edward Eggleston's little nineteenth-century classic, *The Hoosier Schoolmaster* — they were models of democratically elected republicanism. But local oversight promised nothing but trouble to those who wanted national uniformity. That centralization was never likely to happen as long as community boards held sway, with local philosophies and overly sentimentalized personal connections with parents.

Almost at once, even before compulsion had claimed every American state, a process of consolidation began, intended to curb localism. By arranging for larger and larger bureaucratic units, only those with funds enough and reputation to campaign at large beyond the neighborhood could be elected. These mergers were sold as efficiency measures to save taxpayers money, but an oddity occurred — as the districts were enlarged, costs went up, not down, and continued upward in subsequent years. With local watchdogs gone, tendencies to use mass schooling as a cash cow were exploited by every special interest group with political friends.

Inside of a century the number of boards was reduced to 15,000. And each decline in the absolute number of school boards made their composition less and less local. Board seats became stepping stones for the ambitions of politicians, insurance policies for interests which drew their sustenance from school affairs: real estate people, textbook publishers, materials suppliers, et al.

I remember the shock I felt the first time I discovered, quite by accident, that I could personally negotiate larger discounts on book purchases (or anything else) than the school district could. It didn't seem to make sense.[1] The most personally troubling occasion was the moment I decided to use my own funds to purchase classroom sets of good books for student use rather than rely on the "approved" list of books for which school funds could be used, and which required many months, if not a full year, to pass through the acquisition protocols and be shipped. Traveling to a book wholesaler, open to anybody, to secure its standard 40% discount, as I stood at the cash register with a hundred copies of *Moby Dick* and a hundred copies of *Shakespeare's Plays* in shopping carts, the checkout clerk asked me, "Are you a schoolteacher?" Without thinking, I nodded affirmatively, after which she rang the books up at a 25% discount.

"You've made a mistake," I told her. "The discount is 40%."

"Not for schoolteachers," she replied curtly. And when I bellowed in angry protest, she became indignant. "Look," she said, "that's the discount your Board of Education negotiated. If you don't like it, take it up with them."

Now why on earth would my employer sell out my right to a standard discount? Can *you* think of a reason that isn't crooked? And, of course, it wasn't only my right to a full discount the school authorities had stolen, but every teacher's right in New York City. Perhaps this

[1] In one instance, for example, the school board voted to buy 5,000 copies of the *Har-Brace College Handbook* (a grammar/usage guide) for $11.00 a copy at the moment it was being remaindered by the publisher's own book outlet for $1.00 a copy, a $50,000 net difference. When this was pointed out by my wife Janet — a member of the school board at the time who demanded a vote be taken — the balance of the board refused to buy the cheaper copies! Many other examples could be given. Reams of blank paper available for $1.50 a ream in bulk to anyone, were purchased by my school district for $2.50 a ream.

will help you understand why I titled this chapter "Everything You Know about Schools is Wrong."

I remember another moment when I told the assistant principal that I could save him about 40% on the purchase of some world globes and he said without hesitation, "It isn't your money. What are you getting all worked up about?" I realize how cynical that sounds, but here's the paradox: this was a decent man who showed by his daily behavior he actually cared about student welfare.

And the *Har-Brace Handbook* affair? It wasn't arranged by the Tweed gang, but by middle-class neighbors speaking as representatives of a very progressive neighborhood, the Upper West Side of Manhattan, home to Columbia University, the Historical Society, Fordham, the Opera, the Symphony, the Museum of Natural History… and School District Three.

The principle of citizen oversight had become part of the great school illusion, part of the house of mirrors inside which classrooms had been made teacher-proof; schools, principal-proof; school districts, superintendent-proof. Responsibility had migrated elsewhere, but few knew quite where. In any important matters, state departments of education were little better than stooges, the Federal Department of Education — ditto.

In the new world of forced schooling, the training of the young was simply too important a matter to be left to pedagogues, just as had been the situation in ancient Rome. Tracing the word *pedagogue* to its origin in Rome is useful because it leads us to the threshold of the mystery. The Roman *pedagogue* was only a slave, albeit a specialized kind of slave. He was assigned the task of driving home a curriculum created by the Master who owned him, and making sure the pupil got to school on time. But who was the master, and where did he live?

For a compelling answer to that question, you must read Thomas Hobbes' immortal book, *The Leviathan,* written in the first half of the seventeenth century and kept in print ever since. I wouldn't dream of spoiling the surprise you have in store when you discover that the elaborate system of social control official schooling represents has been a vigorously worked out idea for at least 400 years. The real question you should be asking is why, in all the years of school incarceration *you* suffered, did nobody bother to let you in on the secret?

The Fourth Purpose

As the initially transparent motives for schooling were undermined, professionalized pedagogy worked in tandem with government to recommit the institution to the service of corporate economy. Recall that government schooling had been forbidden by default in the federal Constitution, which contains not a single mention of the thing. But the utility it promised for governors — who had no intention of ever honoring a Bill of Rights dedicated to ordinary people — was enormous. Let me select only a few benefits school can offer elites. And let these stand for many more.

Any political management, even tyranny, must provide enough work for ordinary people that revolutionary conditions don't emerge. Forced schooling provides a spectacular jobs project, one almost infinitely elastic, one expanding and contracting with employment needs. It should be no secret to you that institutional schooling, with all its outriggers, is the principal employer in the United States. And such a formidable granter of contracts that even the Defense Department (a similar jobs project) can't keep up.

School is also an efficient way of ensuring loyalty to certain ideas and attitudes; its potential employees can be pre-screened for possession of these, or at the very least for a willingness to conform to them. School is also a tax-absorption mechanism which can claim to be draining resources from the body politic for the good of the next generation, while actually routing a goodly portion of these revenues to friends of the house. My tales of book-buying and materials purchase in School District Three, Manhattan, is only the smallest sample of what is possible. Consider the national school milk purchasing scandal of several decades ago when it was discovered that all over the nation, schools were paying more for milk than retail purchasers!

From its beginnings, forced schooling represented a big step backwards from the exciting free market in learning offered by the bazaar of American life, a market well-illustrated in the lives of Franklin, Jefferson, Farragut, and many others. This asystematic system of learning put the nation on a road to unparalleled power and wealth. And America's young responded brilliantly to it, out-inventing and out-trading every old world competitor by a country mile.

But in the new fashion, different goals were promulgated, goals for which self-reliance, ingenuity, courage, competence, and other frontier virtues became liabilities (because they threatened the authority of management). Under the new system, the goals of good moral values, good citizenship skills, and good personal development were exchanged for a novel fourth purpose — becoming a human resource to be spent by businessmen and politicians. By the end of the nineteenth century, school was looked at by insiders as a branch of industry. In those more innocent times, the creators of schooling were remarkably candid about what they were up to, a candor which shines through a speech delivered in 1909 by Woodrow Wilson to an audience of businessmen in New York City. I mentioned this in the Prologue, but it bears hearing again:

> We want one class to have a liberal education. We want another class, a very much larger class of necessity, to forgo the privilege of a liberal education and fit themselves to perform specific difficult manual tasks.

Forgoing the privilege of education was not to be a matter of choice, which probably explains why Wilson's remarks were not broadcast to the common public but were made behind closed doors. By 1917 all major school administrative jobs nationwide were under control of a group referred to in the press of the day as "the education trust." A record of the first meeting of the trust in Cleveland, Ohio exists, and an attendance roll showing that the interests of Rockefeller and Carnegie were represented, together with those of Harvard, Stanford, the University of Chicago, and the National Education Association. British evolutionist Benjamin Kidd wrote in 1918 that the chief end of the project was "to impose on the young the ideal of subordination."

The Specter of Overproduction

You should be champing at the bit by now demanding to know why all this was being encouraged by the principal families in the nation. Were they so venal and greedy, so saturated with prejudice, that they were willing to sacrifice our revolutionary egalitarian traditions for personal advantage? I'm sure some were, but to say "all" would be to commit a huge oversimplification and a great injustice as well. The folks who gave us forced schooling on the Prussian template were among the finest, most honorable families in the land. Their democratic instincts had been deeply shaken by the biological speculations of Charles Darwin, and by the philosophies of Benedict Spinoza and Johann Fichte (of whom we shall hear specifics in a later chapter), but it took a very down-to-earth, nuts-and-bolts economic idea to seal the fate of hundreds of millions of schoolchildren to come.

The idea went by the name, overproduction, and it's still with us (although now referred to as overcapacity), and it's a very important concept indeed, one whose effects had staggered American prosperity more than once in the nineteenth century. In essence, to overproduce is to make more goods and services for sale than there are customers for those things. When that happens, prices fall. Depending on the degree of overproduction they continue to fall, even below the cost of production. Even so far below costs that the capital required to produce at all is wiped out.

Hidden behind a bonanza for customers when that happens, a dangerous reality lurks: to produce at all in a mass production sense requires huge amounts of money to be assembled from investors for the purchase of production machinery, and for its repair and upgrading, training programs, advertising, a distribution infrastructure, and so on. Unless protection against overproduction is promised investors, why would anyone risk capital to produce in the first place?

What nineteenth century American experience demonstrated unmistakably is that an independent, resourceful, too well-educated common population has the irresistible urge to produce — and the ability to do so. Many famous "panics" of nineteenth century America were caused in part by a hangover from early Federal times and Colonial days when the common ideal was to produce your own food, your own clothing, your own shelter, your own education, your own medical care, your own entertainment, etc. The common population was still insufficiently conditioned to be interdependent and specialized.

And added to this burden of self-sufficiency (from a corporate point of view) was the incredible *inventiveness* of the American people, a natural by-product of three factors: an open-source learning tradition; a heterogeneous, mixed-age society which didn't exclude the young from full participation; and a government presence without heavy-handedness. Given this heady brew, inventions poured out of the American population with dazzling speed, at a pace unknown in the rest of the world's experience. Unexpected invention is probably the easiest way to provoke the creative destruction which ends the career of otherwise dominant enterprises under capitalism. Ideas are just as deadly in overproduction as hats are, or bushels of corn.

From 1880 to 1930, the term "overproduction" was heard everywhere, in boardrooms, elite universities, gentlemen's clubs, and highbrow magazines. It was a demon which had to be locked in the dungeon. And rationalized pedagogy was a natural vehicle to implant habits and attitudes to accomplish that end. Under this outlook, the classroom would never be used to produce knowledge, but only to consume it; it would not encourage the confined to produce ideas, only to consume the ideas of others. The ultimate goal implanted in student minds, which replaced the earlier goal of independent livelihoods, was getting a good job.

I don't mean to be crazy about this, the new school institution served other purposes, too; but seeing the connection between long-term legal confinement of children and the nation's business gives us an essential perspective in rethinking the role of mass schooling. Classical business values corrupt education, they have no place in education except as cultural artifacts to be examined.

For the first two centuries of our existence, such an institution would have been unthinkable — the young were too valuable a part of economic and social reality. Indispensable, in fact. But when the young were assigned to consume, not produce; when they were ordered to be passive, not active, as part of the general society, the schools we have were the inevitable result of this transformation. As soon as you understand the functions it was given to perform in the new corporate economy, nothing about school at all should surprise you. Not even its Columbine moments.

2

Walkabout: London

Author's Note:
I've spoken about 1,500 times since I quit schoolteaching, in every American state and twelve foreign countries, but only two audience members in all that time were so provoked to anger by what I said that they screamed insults at me from their seats. One, in 1992, was the son of a very famous economist from California, and the other, in 1998 (if memory serves), was a very famous stock speculator in New York. The reason I'm telling you this is that the substance of this chapter, albeit with somewhat different details, is what drove those men to rage. So you've been warned.

The idea I'll be arguing here — that free-form "education," the variety I call "open-source" education, is of much higher quality than rule-driven, one-size-fits-all, "testable" schooling — came to me first as a teenage boy when an amazing thing happened to my beloved Uncle Bud Zimmer. I think you'll see what I mean when I tell you Bud's miracle.

Prior to WWII, Bud was a steelworker and a deckhand on the paddlewheel river steamers which went from Pittsburgh to New Orleans. He was a tough, tough young man, looked a lot like John Wayne in *Stagecoach*, and the ladies loved him. But he was a high-school dropout. He enlisted to go to war in 1942 when I was seven, and I saw the troop train carry him off one night. Somehow he qualified for Officer's Candidate School, and was eventually shipped off to Europe to join the invasion as a lieutenant. In his platoon was an enlisted man, Al Rockwell, who would one day be heir to the Rockwell Manufacturing empire. Mr. Rockwell, a man of strong libertarian principles, insisted on going into combat as an enlisted soldier. They became friends.

I can't remember what ordinary jobs Bud held when he came back from the war as a captain, but I do know his CV didn't include a college degree. One day he called me on the phone from Cincinnati, and said that before I went to Cornell he wanted me to work for him "at a real job," to "stop sponging off your parents and earn your own money." What job did he have in mind? He said, "I want you to load 125-pound slabs of steel onto boxcars from nine to five every day. I want you to live with me near the Rockwell plant in Ohio and pay room and board. How's that sound?"

It turned out that Bud was the manager of the plant, employing thousands. "I have two dozen Harvard hotshots working for me," he said. "They'll do anything I want: shine my shoes, wax my car, but I can't let them see me favoring my nephew, so I'll have to work you twice as hard as anyone else. Is that OK?"

A real job with a grown-up's pay at 16? For that, anything would have been OK! I was too unworldly at the time to even think of the big mystery — how on Earth could a common steelworker *without an education* be ordering Harvard graduates around? And running a huge industrial plant? My mistake was thinking of Bud as a man without an education. He had a superb education: it was only schooling he lacked.

~

Jonathan Goodwin

Google the cover of *Fast Company* magazine for November 2007, and you'll be staring into the unremarkable face of junior high-school dropout Jonathan Goodwin. How does a young fellow from a poor Kansas farm family rate such treatment? No high school, no college. After bailing out of seventh grade at age thirteen, Jonathan did odd jobs at a local garage. Pitiful pay. No future in that, right?

"That was my school," he told *Fast Company*.

When the price squeeze in gas came, it puzzled Jonathan. It seemed phony to him. He knew technology existed which could give cars 60 to 100 miles per gallon, and push emissions near zero. Why didn't Detroit offer it?

No matter. Jonathan could build it himself. And before you could say "crazy kid!" he had more business than he could handle, charging up to $25,000 to convert a Hummer. It didn't hurt him that one of his best customers was Arnold Schwartzenegger, governor of California. And a one-time dropout himself.

Jonathan is taking in over a million a year doing four conversions a month. Before he was old enough to vote, he was a self-reliant human being adding value to the community. When he left seventh grade he was just a little older than America's first admiral, David Farragut was when he took command of a captured British ship off the coast of Peru in the War of 1812, at the age of 12 — and sailed it to Boston; the same age George Washington was when he dropped out of schooling; the same age as Thomas Jefferson when as a young man Thomas began to manage a large plantation and 250 employees in Virginia (both his parents being deceased). The same age you and I were once, sitting at our school desks, copying notes from a blackboard, getting yelled at.

Danica Patrick

On April 20, 2008, Danica Patrick, age 26, became the first woman in big-time auto-racing history ever to win a major event. She was driving against two-time Indy 500 winner Helio Castroneves, and roared past him in the final two laps of the Motegi, Japan 300, and won going away. "This is about finding something you love and following through with it," she told reporters after the race.

Ten years earlier, at age 16, Danica dropped out of high school and went to London, all by herself, to learn to sustain high speeds for hours at a time. You might have been in high school at 16, probably a sophomore, looking forward to a graduation far far away.

Nick Schulman

Nick Schulman, age 21, is a neighbor of mine in Manhattan, although we've never met. Had I stayed in teaching, it's likely Nick would have attended my junior high school; he might even have been in my eighth-grade English class, although he probably wouldn't have been there very often, because it was in eighth grade that Nick became a truant, cutting classes to play pool. Not a good sign, right? When he found computer games, he dropped out of school. At age 18, in 2005, he became a poker addict. Pity his poor mother. Other kids were worrying about SATs and college, but Nick was worrying about straights and flushes.

On February 28, 2008, the *New York Post* devoted a split page to Nick. He had just won two million dollars on the world poker tour. Now that the problem of paying rent was taken care of, he was "ready for a different kind of fulfillment," he told the paper. Philosophy was what Nick had his sights set on now, and for that he planned to enroll in college. That's where you probably were at 21, too. Without the two million.

Diablo Cody

If your teenage daughter changed her name to "Diablo," you might shrug it off as a passing fancy. But if she came home one day with the announcement that her life's ambition was to be a stripper, and to prove it she created a pornographic blog called "Pussy Ranch," you might begin to worry.

In her mid-twenties, now a lap dancer, Diablo published a book about her degrading and dangerous work, called *Candy Girl,* and two years later, in a cut-to-the-thigh leopard-print gown (with a gigantic tattoo of a stripper covering her right arm and shoulder), she stepped onstage at the Oscar ceremonies in Hollywood to accept her own Oscar for best screenplay. Her movie was *Juno,* about a pregnant, unmarried teen facing the future with courage.

Diablo Cody told the audience, "Most of all I want to thank my family for loving me exactly the way I am." In the linear logic of pedagogy, Diablo was way off the recommended track, but in the different universe of open-source learning, which operates through experimentation and personal feedback loops instead of expert advice, she was right on point.

Open-Source Learning

Jonathan, Danica, Nick, Diablo. Each took an open-source road to an individualized education under personal management, exactly as Ben

Franklin once did. Open-source learning accepts that everything under the sun might be a possible starting point on the road to self-mastery and a good life — garage work, poker, lap dancing, whatever. In open source, sequences are personally designed or personally signed off on. And everyone you encounter is a potential teacher: garage mechanics, card sharps, lap dancers, race car drivers, everyone.

Potter Stewart, the former Supreme Court Justice, once remarked he couldn't define pornography, but he knew it when he saw it. Open-source is like that. To hedge it in with official algorithms is to ruin it, but I owe you at least a rough abstract: in open source, *teaching is a function*. Not a profession. Anyone with something to offer can teach. The student determines who is or is not a teacher, not the government. In open source, you don't need a license to teach any more than Socrates did. Right there you can feel how different the basic assumptions of open source are. No student faces failure for deciding not to learn from you.

In open source, students are active initiators. It all sounds too undisciplined, I know, but life beyond schooling is exactly like that. You either write your own script, or you become an actor in somebody else's script.

Shen Wenrong

The *Financial Times* of March 17, 2006, tells the story of a silent contest between college-trained executives and engineers, and a band of Chinese peasants. Since the account has real bearing on this idea of open-source learning, let me summarize it for you.

Not long ago, the ThyssenKrupp Corporation of Germany decided to unload its mighty "Phoenix" steel plant in Dortmund. Steel prices were down, and it looked to management as if they would stay down, so the decision was made to sell all 220 acres of buildings to China, even though that would throw 10,000 Germans out of work.

Management expected two payoffs: one in the sales price, and one in the bill to move the plant from Dortmund to near Shanghai. ThyssenKrupp estimated that would take three years and an army of specialists. China bought Phoenix, but choked on the moving bill. They would do the job themselves.

One fine day a raggedy band of a thousand peasants led by peasant Shen Wenrong showed up in Dortmund. Here's a capsule of data to help you think about Mr. Shen: He didn't use a computer. He didn't have a real office. He worked from behind something looking suspiciously like a kid's school desk. Shen's first computer-less, office-less decision was to avoid German housing and meal costs. In three weeks, his crew built its own dormitories and commissary.

Then it broke the steel plant down. Crated it. Shipped it to China. Uncrated it. And set it back up, inside of *one* year, not three. Numerous rules were broken in the process whenever more creative problem-solving seemed appropriate.

In the time it took to move Phoenix, China's huge orders for steel on world markets drove prices through the roof, exactly as China's planners had calculated would happen. Phoenix in China was a big money-maker from the beginning, just as it would have been if left in Germany. So the ignorant Chinese not only worked harder than the Germans, they had better judgement, too.

How were we ever tricked into believing that specialists are needed for matters well within the reach of ordinary people? How did we come to think so little of ourselves? If unschooled peasants can demolish and re-erect a steel plant three times faster than professionals, then you and I need to re-examine everything we've been conditioned to accept as truth. Everything. That's called dialectical thinking. Once dialectics was central to school, but we don't teach it anymore. Not even to the so-called gifted and talented.

Walkabout: London

High-school dropout, Sir Richard Branson, thinks the important lesson of his life happened at the age of four. It was a London walkabout, as he tells of it in his autobiography, and tells once again in *The New Yorker* (May 2007). It happened this way: four-year-old Richard was on a drive with mother Eve in the London suburb of Shamley

Green, miles from home, in an area where Richard had never been. Eve pulled over and asked him whether he thought he could find his way home from where they were.

He said yes, whereupon she told him to get out and do so then. "Mother was determined to make us independent," he told the magazine. By age twelve he was making hundred-mile round-trip bike rides alone to the beach at Bournemouth. After a brief go at high school, Branson dropped out, never spending a day in college. At nineteen, his first successful business was launched. Virgin Airlines, his music business, and many others were in the near future, as was his announcement that he would construct a private space vehicle. On July 29, 2008, a picture of Branson, mother Eve, and his completed rocket appeared on the front page of newspapers around the world. Some 250 seats for the maiden voyage were all snapped up at $200,000 a piece.

Is four too young to become involved in serious business? Tiger Woods was sinking putts on the Mike Douglas television show at age two, so I tend to doubt it.

Glen Doman

I remember sitting in Glen Doman's office at the Institutes for the Achievement of Human Potential on Stenton Avenue in Philadelphia about twenty years ago, looking at framed tributes on his walls from the famous of the planet such as Jackie Kennedy, while Glen explained how easy it was to teach a baby to read, count, and do basic arithmetical functions.

"They learn instantly," he said, "the trouble comes if you wait until they're five, or if you spend too much time in review. Every year you delay increases the magnitude of difficulty." Doman has sold three million copies of his book, *Teach Your Baby to Read*, although you're not likely to find a single copy in a school.

I went to visit Doman for an odd reason. My daughter, then at MIT, told me he was the laughing stock of her friends. She said it in a phone call from Cambridge, and the minute we finished speaking, I

I dialed Philadelphia information, got the number at The Institutes, and rang him up, although we had no prior association. We were total strangers to one another. I asked if someday I might visit to see the alleged miracle myself.

"What are you doing this evening?" he said. An hour later I was driving to Philadelphia, where I met Glen in the late evening, stayed in a guest bedroom, and next morning was watching his school in operation. It was a place with no entrance requirements. Glen took anybody who applied. It was a place where seven-year-olds read real books and grown-up magazines for pleasure. Impromptu, the kids decided to put on a scene from *The Mikado* for my pleasure, complete with song and dance. I left with a heightened sense of just how far official schooling has dumbed us down.

The Human Genome Project

Branson's successful walkabout and the dirt-farmer savvy of Shen are only possible to people with access to the classroom of the greater world. All my life I've been saturated with warnings of how people without diplomas, certificates, and "credentials" are ruined, doomed to insignificance. You've been warned too, I know.

So how are we to account for Washington and Lincoln, our two best presidents, having almost no school between them? How to explain America's two legendary industrialists, Carnegie and Rockefeller, both being elementary school dropouts? I mean, why didn't school matter in their day, but only in ours? Is this open-source thing feasible in the modern high-tech sciences? If you think not, tell me how we got the human genome map from a horrible student, surfer-bum named Craig Venter and a born-again Christian homeschooler named Frances Collins, who studied whatever he wanted growing up, and for as long as he wanted to study it — no attempt at a balanced intellectual diet, or any rigorous discipline imposed from outside. Collins told the *New York Times* a few years back that Virginia authorities would have thrown his mom in jail if they knew what school looked like in the Collins home.

A Torch Singer at MIT

On April 27, 2007, national headlines announced the firing of MIT's famous director of admissions, Merilee Jones. Jones was dismissed in disgrace after 28 years of outstanding service during which MIT had granted her its highest honors and she had become a heroine of the college admissions world nationally

Jones specialized in female recruitment, not an easy sell at a tech school, but during her tenure she tripled the number of women enrolled. At the time of her dismissal, the press quoted students and faculty with characterizations of her service ranging from "beloved" to "irreplaceable." So why had she been canned? Had to be molesting students or something serious like that, right?

You'd never guess in a million years, so I might as well tell you. When MIT hired her, Jones lied on her job application about having three college degrees. Actually, she had been a nightclub singer in country bars in upstate New York.

Philip Clay, MIT's chancellor, told the press such a mistake would never happen again. No more nightclub singers! "In future..." said Clay (you can almost hear him clearing his throat), "In future we will take a big lesson from this experience."

When I read that I asked myself what lesson could possibly be learned from throwing away a brilliant colleague whose worth was proven, not theoretical? Was the lesson that doing a sensational job is insufficient job protection? For me, the lesson was that Clay himself should be fired.

Ingvar Kamprad

Degrees should never stand as proxies for education. Think of Ingvar Kamprad, diagnosed as dyslexic by self-proclaimed school experts in Sweden. He began independent life selling fish from a bicycle, without a degree. Bit by bit he added matches and xmas decorations to his inventory. What a hard life! How much better it would have been if he had gone through several colleges and become an investment banker at Bear Stearns. But as Ingvar's line of wares grew, a powerful idea began to drive him, the idea of a store dedicated to bringing beauty and utility at low cost, to everyone. This dyslexic fish peddler is worth 31 billion dollars at the moment, as the founder of IKEA, and more important than that money — which he'll never live long enough to spend — the flame of his determination to add value to the lives of others still burns brightly.

The Graduate

You're on the road to being educated when you know yourself so thoroughly you write your own script instead of taking a part written by others. A migrant fruit picker named Charles Webb fits this description for me. You've very likely consumed a piece of Webb's imagination, if not the fruit, if you've ever seen the classic American film *The Graduate.* Webb sold millions of copies of the book, and his film became a beacon to an entire generation of American young people. It's theme, that a life built around buying things is a disaster, helped turn the film into a runaway hit, still shown and still rented years later. Charles and his wife made millions and were on every A-team guest list from Easthampton to Maui.

As their life turned into the non-life of perpetual celebrity and celebrity projects, Webb and his wife made the copyright over to the Anti-Defamation League, gave their entire fortune away, and set out as vagabonds in a trailer, at one time becoming migrants picking fruit in California.

"Wealth didn't work for us," he said.

Dropouts

Every single school day in America, 7,000 students drop out, some confused, some angry, but all are brave. If we had the sense our ancestors did, we'd look on these dropouts as a grand resource, as people whose minds the standard programming couldn't tame. We'd treat them with respect. One and a quarter million people a year, perhaps more, with potential not necessarily inferior to Ben Franklin, the dropout, or Branson, the dropout, or the dropout Wright brothers, or slum urchin Lula da Silva, grown to the presidency of Brazil without a certificate and on the verge of making his country the first major nation to be free of petroleum out of the ground.

What does it say to us that a million and a quarter young people a year don't want to be in classrooms, don't want to be there so much they're willing to endure scorn, insult, and constant discrimination as the price of escape? Are they just unfortunates who have earned a future of misery, or is it we, the self-imprisoned and perpetually frightened, waving our wallets and homes in the burbs as evidence we must be alive, who are the truly miserable? Year after year the International Happiness Survey ranks our country as among the mediocre in happiness, along with Germany and every other Anglo-Saxon country. Does the phony pecking order created by degrees, and by elite colleges like Yale and Stanford, have anything to do with this?

Wake up! If things were really as you've been conditioned to believe, how could slum urchin Lula govern a complex modern nation? How could lower-middle-class semi-urchin Adolf Hitler have risen to command the best-schooled nation in history? How could Thomas Edison have dropped out of elementary school, gone west alone with no money or contacts, and by age 15 be enjoying multiple streams of revenue and be earning four times the wages of a skilled workman?

How could penniless elementary school dropout Edison grow up on his own in a working-class environment, invent the electric light, the phonograph, win 1,003 patents, and build General Electric? Edison had contempt for college graduates and discriminated against them in hiring all his life.

If school were the life-and-death matter you've always been told, none of this could have happened. How could George Bernard Shaw drop out of school at 14 and teach himself to be the greatest dramatist of the 20th century? Why has no school, no college, no politician, no foundation, no social thinker ever connected the dots for you as I just did?

Another Inconvenient Truth

In 2006, the University of Connecticut set out to discover how much learning happens in a student between entering as freshmen and graduating as a senior. Five academic areas were selected to measure, using 14,000 students at 50 American colleges, including Yale, Brown, and Georgetown. At 16 of those 50 — including Yale, Brown, and Georgetown — graduating seniors knew less than incoming freshmen. Negative growth had occurred. In the other 34, no measurable change had taken place

A bald summary might look like this: after spending an average of six years in search of a BA degree or its equivalent, and spending an average of a quarter million in cash and loans, a great many young people had nothing or even less than nothing to show for the investment. What they had was a piece of magical paper. This is a script out of the Marx Brothers.

John Kanzius

On April 13, 2008, television show *Sixty Minutes* reported a heretofore unknown method of killing cancer had been invented by a patient with no background in science and no college degree. Nobel Prize–winning cancer researcher Rick Smalley said that it was the most impressive development he had ever seen in his life, that it "would change medicine forever."

The Kanzius method destroys tumors without chemotherapy, surgery, or familiar radiation. After 36 rounds of chemo, John Kanzius was desperate enough to wrack his own brains for something which the cancer empire had missed, and he found such a thing in memories of his boyhood hobby as a radio hobbyist. As a kid, Kanzius had been intrigued by a curious fact: that when harmless radio waves passed through metal, the metal heated up. Was it possible that a tumor injected with metal particles could be killed by passing radio waves through it? Ridiculous idea, isn't it? Had it merit, surely the army of trained scientists who cost the nation tens of billions every year would have found it, wouldn't they?

He tested his theory in his garage, using a machine he constructed out of used pie tins. Sure enough, when the bottom of a weiner was injected with metal and shot with radio waves, the bottom cooked but the top remained cool. Kanzius passed his findings on to university laboratories, which reported back that in preliminary tests radio waves did, indeed, kill cancers.

No formula known could have predicted John Kanzius. How many more of him are there out there, denied a voice in our synthetic anti-meritocracy which awards privilege on the basis of college degrees and family connections? One more Kanzius? Ten more? Ten million more? An inconceivable number?

Listen friends, if peasants can deconstruct steel mills, torch singers can revolutionize admissions at high-tech colleges, junior high dropouts can get 100 miles to the gallon, beach-bum surfers can map the human genome, tiny women can blast through the male monopoly of big-time auto racing, dyslexic fish peddlars can establish global merchandising empires, and lap dancers can win Oscars for scriptwriting, some vitally important piece is missing in the conventional way schools treat learning and accomplishment.

Twenty years ago I was talking to some Amish fellows in Barnesville, Ohio, about our ridiculous space program and its waste of scarce resources. One Amish man said they had talked about building a moon rocket once, and all agreed it would be an easy thing to do, but why would anyone except a damn fool *want* to do it? If that sounds like hot air, you want to remember Richard Branson.

~

The Artificial Extension of Childhood

The same young people we confine to classrooms these days once cleared this continent when it was a wilderness, built roads, canals, cities; whipped the greatest military power of earth not once but twice, sold ice to faraway India before refrigeration, and produced so many miracles — from the six-shooter to the steamboat to manned flight — that America spread glimmerings of what open-source creativity could do all around the planet.

In those days Americans weren't burdened by a concept of the phony stage of life called "adolescence," or any other artificial extension of childhood. About the age of seven you added value to the world around you, or you were a parasite. Like all sane people, so-called kids wanted to grow up as soon as possible — that's why old photos show boys and girls looking like men and women. All that takes is carrying your share of the load, and a few open-source adventures and presto! You *are* grown up. In Ben Franklin's day when you were ready to take your turn, no pseudo-sciences out of Germany stood in your way.

The pre-Civil War American economy was dominated by independent livelihoods, and even after the war, for another fifty years or so, young men (who would be called "boys" today) like Andrew Carnegie could start life as an elementary school dropout at the age of seven, and be partners in business with the president of the Pennsylvania Railroad at age 20. Are similar lives being fashioned today? Of course they are, but it isn't considered wise to talk about it openly anymore. Think of Shawn Fanning with his millions from starting Napster at age 18, and Fanning is far from alone — it's just that those lucky ones allowed to do it are far more discreet in our time.

An earlier America celebrated accomplishment and shrewdness from any source. Kids weren't locked away to provide employment for millions. America had room for anyone with energy, brass, and ideas. Foreign visitors like Tocqueville and DuPont de Nemours were constantly being dazzled by the high energy released in a society reaching for revolutionary egalitarianism, one which mixed all ages together, took risks, and discarded the rigid categories of European tradition.

Our Civil War changed everything for the worse. Forget the propaganda you heard in school, it had nothing to do with slavery. By 1860 Europe had already abandoned the slave institution, and the United States was very close to doing the same — it wouldn't have lasted twenty more years, for many reasons, most interesting of which, for me, is the simple fact that wage-slaves, free in name only, are much cheaper to exploit, and work harder than slaves.

As soon as you put the red herring of slavery out of mind, the contest between family and nature as centers of meaning (versus profit achieved by converting human beings into human resources) becomes clear. Northern industrialists were already privy to the power and fortune being earned converting large populations in Britain, Germany, and elsewhere from a yeomanry into a proletariat. They lusted after similar advantages, but were sophisticated enough to realize that the American traditions of independence, self-reliance, ingenuity, family, and religious worship would have to be marginalized first before this transformation could successfully be worked. Compulsory school laws to break up family closeness were a big part of the package in Germany, and that German magic was coveted in the drawing rooms of New York and Boston.

In the industrial state which emerged rampant in the wake of the Civil War, the entrepreneurial egalitarianism of the original American design was put to death by factories and licensing laws, government interventions and requirements, and eventually by forced schooling. By 1880, factories and financiers ruled the American roost, and a professional proletariat of academics, lawyers, politicians, and others dependent on the favor of the mighty were making it hot for Americans who fought to maintain a libertarian nation as promised by the Declaration and the Bill of Rights. With this radical transformation from local democracy to *de facto* oligarchy, people with minds of their own became an impediment to efficient management. Think of it this way: lives assigned to routine work are best kept childish.

Childish people are not only obedient (if we discount their occasional tantrums), but they make the best consumers because they have little natural sales resistance. Since Plato, a stream of utopian writers has worked to give management recipes to cook childish lives; lives susceptible to the will of their betters.

Take a second to think about these utopian algorithms — dividing people from one another and from their natural allies, is right at the head of the list, but all require wiping the slate as clean of close emotional ties — even ties to yourself! — as possible. Family, deep friendships, church, culture, tradition, anything which might contradict the voice of authority, is suspect. An independent mind is the worst danger of all, but twelve years spent in a school chair (and now in front of a computer terminal or television, etc.), will convert the most crowded inner life into a virtually blank slate.

The *trouble* with open-source learning, as far as policymakers are concerned, is that it almost guarantees an independent mind and character will develop — not a cosmetic simulation of those things, which schooling cultivates. Even worse, taking charge of mixing your own education leads to a healthy self-regard — and confident folks are considerably less manageable than anxious ones.

So, in the managerial utopia which came to be planned on policy levels after the Southern side of our national dialectic was broken by Civil War, training of the young had to be pre-empted, or nearly so, and nets of rules had to replace the trial-and-error feedback loops of open source. Andrew Carnegie, one of the principal architects of the new command-and-control system saw its drawbacks clearly; he said it would act to some degree as an anti-meritocracy, denying a goodly number of the best quality people in every field the leadership their merit should have earned them — but on the whole Carnegie thought it was a fair bargain: exchanging merit for social stability and protection of capital.

America's first national commissioner of education, eminent Hegelian scholar William Torrey Harris, said in a long essay in 1906 entitled "The Philosophy of Education," that a prime purpose of the new institutional schooling was to teach *self-alienation* (in the interests of state and corporate security), and that this could be best accomplished in dark, airless corridors. It never fails to amaze me how people can hear words like that — and the school trail is littered with them — and ignore them, as if they were only idle talk.

It's time, I think, to face some basic truth: highly centralized mass production economies take on the character of oligarchies, they can't allow *natural* processes of capitalism to go unregulated; the creative destruction which Schumpeter saw as central to the health of market economoies can't be allowed to occur naturally. That's what the expression "too big to be allowed to fail" heard so frequently these days, along with its corollary, "bail-out" should signal to anyone with a modicum of economic training. The United States is now only nominally a free market economy; corporate welfare is dominant, the enormous American military has not, for a very long time, been primarily about protecting common American citizens from harm. It exists for several never-discussed reasons: to provide employment for the underclasses; to avoid uprisings at home; to act as a centrifuge in distributing wealth through contracts back to the managers of the system and their allies; and it exists, in the gravest extreme to "go domestic," an expression heard often at officer training facilities around the country, one well-illustrated by the now-legendary paramilitary interventions at Waco and Ruby Ridge.

Highly centralized mass production economies can't function well without colonizing individual minds and converting them into a mass mind. The conversion works best if started early, in the lower grades of elementary school, in kindergarten and pre-kindergarten. The function of these collective rituals we call school has very little to do with intellectual development — consider only the familiar madness of teaching the colors and days of the week or months of the year to little people who come to school already knowing those things. The collective rituals of lower grades are about habit training, about practicing attention and fealty to authority. In this way, independent consciousness can be undermined in its formative stages.

The opposite of mass-mindedness is dialectical-mindedness. A tremendous example of this is buried in the foundational religious documents of Western culture, in the story of young Jesus closely questioning elders in the temple after slipping away from his parents, itself a contrarian action. Indeed, the New Testament is so replete with contrarianism it's little wonder it plays no part in institutional schooling, although it plays a stupendous part in Western history from the beginning of the modern era until today.

Complex minds are always dialectical. Aristotle sets that as a basic requirement of being fully human, but because the reality of dialectical minds is that they always challenge assumptions and take nothing for granted, their presence in large numbers poses acute problems for corporate business and corporate government.

Take the matter of personal *production* as opposed to *consumption;* production of goods, values, ideas, and marching orders. Colonial and early federal America held the ideal of self-sufficiency as the very pinnacle of achievement. The ideal household aimed to produce its own food, clothing, shelter, entertainment, transportation, medical care, education, child care, and social security. A large fraction of the population never got there, but as a City on the Hill to strive for it was an ennobling vision which some families, especially on the frontier, succeeding in making happen. It was this idea of being personally empowered, in contrast to the servile states of Europe and Asia, which acted as a magnet for the world's peoples — not the prospect of two cars, a house in the suburbs, and the latest computer junk.

Were that vision to have been maintained through forced schooling, it would have destroyed corporations in embryo. Overproduction would have strangled capital accumulation by posing continuous competition — and without capital accumulation, no dominant corporations. Far from *production* as an ideal, it was *consumption* that had to be encouraged. School had to train in consumption habits: listening to others, moving on a bell or horn signal without questioning, becoming impressionable — more accurately, gullible — in order to do well on tests. Kids who insisted on producing their own lives had to be humiliated publicly as a warning to others.

Producing yourself is the ultimate form of production. For many years America's promise to the rest of the world's peoples was that if they could only manage to get here, no feudal order would thwart that dream. But after the Civil War, the argument between entrepreneurial values — which inevitably celebrate open-source learning — and industrial values — by their nature feudal — was over.

When the smoke cleared fifty years later, the imitation sciences of pedagogy and psychology had been imported from northern Germany, pressed into service through the school institution to create a proletariat: family-less, land-less people with only weak ties to religion, tradition, or culture. Even the middle management and professional strata are best seen as a proletariat, too — a professionalized proletariat — only lightly rooted in its relationships to people, places, or principles.

To enlist public opinion behind this utopian transformation, a pathological state of youth, heretofore unrecognized by history, was designed by G. Stanley Hall of Johns Hopkins University. He called it *adolescence* and debuted the condition in a huge two-volume study of that name, published in 1904. Trained in Prussia as behavioral psychologist Wilhelm Wundt's first assistant, Hall (immensely influential in school circles at the beginning of the 20th century) identified adolescence as a dangerously irrational state of human growth requiring psychological controls inculcated through schooling.

As John Dewey's mentor at German-inspired Hopkins, Hall's invention seemed to justify the extension of state schooling into the teen years, institutionalizing the most productive fraction of humanity for psychological treatment — in confinement with poorly educated employees of the state given a virtual monopoly over training the young.

In this dazzling coup, the teenagers who had helped build the new nation were now officially deprived of fully engaged lives such as Edison or Carnegie had once enjoyed.

A managerial class having forcefully emerged in America, the Anglo-Saxon strong class system was now being imposed on the United States through forced schooling. Walt Whitman once said, "Only Hegel is fit for America," and now, following Hegel's instructions, history itself was being slowed down, the brakes put on change — by crippling the American arguments among ideas, peoples, sections, religions — through one-size-fits-all schooling. The hope for unending argument had been built into our very founding documents, into the guarantees of free speech and access to deadly weaponry given common citizens. Our division of powers — an executive, two houses of Congress, and a high court — a division which defies engineering wisdom in its structural inefficiency — was meant to preserve argument as the best protection for common citizens.

Power was to be kept decentralized in the original conception of the United States, and experts kept in their place: decision-making was for ordinary people, not specialists. But now, all that careful, all that caringly thoughtful architecture which made America so unique, was to be put to death through bulk-process, psychological schooling, imposed by force. I urge you to examine in your own mind the assumptions which must lie behind using the police power to insist that once-sovereign spirits have no choice but to submit to being schooled by strangers. Surely this is one of the most radical acts in human history, not the least of its breathtakingly radical assertions being that you must attend *for your own good!* It is the most striking evidence of the Teutonic mind at work behind the façade of everyday schooling.

Prior to the heavy-duty interventions of social engineering into the growing-up time, America — open-source educated for two hundred years — was a spectacularly resourceful and inventive society. One need only read the many journals written by early foreign visitors (Tocqueville's being the most prominent), to see how earth-shaking the liberty given to ordinary Americans really was. Nothing like the creative energy being released had ever been seen before, or was even dreamed of as possible. With few exceptions, invention is the province of youthful insight; cut that spring of ideas off by embedding the young in a network of rules and judgements, and you should expect important negative consequences.

Shortly after adolescence was professionalized, a decline in the numbers of patent applications by Americans occurred. After WWII, when institutionalized schooling including college and kindergarten grew by leaps and bounds, that decline accelerated. Universal schooling had weakened the imagination, just as Spinoza predicted it would in 1690, and Fichte predicted in the second decade of the 19th century. Of course, both those men were heartily in favor of that weakening; their school schemes were for the benefit of the "best" people. But if those relative ancients could work out the school mechanism and its negative effects long before it existed, surely you can, too.

Why would anybody *want* to do this? That's easy: imaginative individuals are notoriously unmanageable and unpredictable, because they are irrepressibly inventive.

The Honor Roll

Craig Venter, the beach bum surfer who shared the laurels for producing the map of the human genome, was born in 1946. He found school exquisitely boring and took vengeance by driving teachers crazy. He cut class often to hit the boogie board and only escaped junior high school because a teacher changed one of his "F" grades to "D–" so the school could be rid of him.

Venter enlisted in the navy, serving as a medical corpsman in Vietnam. There he learned to despise bureaucracy with its books of rules in place of allowing adaptation to unique situations. His autobiography, *A Life Decoded,* adds many details to this skeletal outline, but suffice it to say he was hardly anyone's likely candidate for scientific immortality. Nor could Franklin Roosevelt have been predicted, from his "C" average in high school, and his "C" average in college.

George W. Bush had a "C" average in high school and a "C" average in college (which won't surprise most of you), but that it was a higher "C" in both high school and college than was earned by Massachusetts Senator John Kerry, probably *will* surprise you. Al Gore flunked out of his first college and squeaked through his second with a "C–" average; Dick Cheney, vice-president as a I speak, flunked out too. Legendary progressive Senator Paul Wellstone scored 800 on his *combined* SATs.

US global computer dominance came from men without college degrees: Bill Gates and Paul Allen of Microsoft — no college degrees. Steve Jobs and Steve Wozniak of Apple — no college degrees. (After Wozniak was already a mega-billionaire, he took a degree to give himself eligibility to teach elementary school in California, I've been told. But that college *made* Wozniak is clearly untrue.) Michael Dell is another un-degreed immortal of the computer game, as is Larry Ellison of Oracle.

Ted Turner, founder of CNN, dropped out of college in his freshman year; William Faulker's high school grades were too horrible to get him into the University of Mississippi, but after service as an officer in WWI, he was given a waiver and enrolled. In Faulkner's first (and last) term, he received a "D" in English and dropped out in disgust, never to return. Warren Avis, the man who pioneered auto rentals at airports, decided college was a waste of time and never even applied. Edward Hamilton, the nation's largest independent mail-order book dealer, wrote me that the advantage he had over his competition at the beginning was that he hadn't wasted his capital or time on college. Paul Orfalea, the highly intelligent, soft-spoken founder of Kinko's, was not regarded as very bright by his high school, as he tells in his memoir *Copy This*. Shawn Fanning, whose invention of Napster at age 18 almost ruined the commercial music industry, was hired by that industry in 2007 for millions of dollars, to design a plan to save it. Shawn had no college degree, and currently has no plans to get one.

Lew Wasserman

Lew Wasserman created modern Hollywood almost single-handedly with his colossal MCA talent agency; he had no college and virtually no seat-time in high school, although he did "earn" a diploma, although not in the customary fashion.

Starting at age 13, Wasserman quit school, working instead as a movie usher on Hollywood Boulevard. He was trusted sufficiently to be given keys to open the theater in the afternoon. That privilege gave him an idea how to get a diploma without attending class, through a trade with the school principal. On Wasserman's part, he would smuggle out prints of the latest films from the theater, get them to the high school long before the movie opened, screen them for a low admission fee for students, give the money to the principal to buy band instruments and football equipment, then rush the prints back to the theater before anyone arrived, with no one the wiser. That's called *quid pro quo.* He was 13 when he began to employ that ancient Roman principle.

With the time saved by not copying from the blackboard, Wasserman used the hours to think up brilliant show business contracts which are still studied in law schools as models of the genre. With those contracts, he signed stars like Fred Astaire and the Gish sisters into his new MCA stable.

Warren Buffet

Warren Buffet started in business at the age of 6, selling iced Coca-Colas door-to-door in un-airconditioned Omaha, Nebraska one hot summer during the Depression.

Steadily he added other businesses to his string: selling lost golf balls to the club pro shop; sifting discarded race track betting tickets for winners accidentally thrown away; designing a system which allowed him to deliver 1,500 newspapers on one delivery route; renting pinball machines to barber shops. From age 13 he supported himself, and by 18 Buffet had the equivalent of $100,000 in the bank. Then he applied to Wharton Business School. and was turned down.

What Buffet learned open source, by active risk-taking, imagination, and real work, schools either cannot or will not teach. It's fair to ask "why not?" Why don't schools anywhere get into the minutiae of opportunity and self-sufficiency? Why do they keep selling "a good job" as the end of the school road when, as many Americans like the Lancaster Amish still believe, no "job" is worth giving up your independence for, at least not for very long?

Consider what society would look like if 65 million trapped schoolchildren learning to be consumers were suddenly set to actively imagining themselves in independent livelihoods, adding value to the rest of the community; imagining themselves as producers instead of bored consumers. Wouldn't we soon be overrun with Buffets, Venters, Wassermans, Danica Patricks and Diablo Codys? Isn't that exactly what America needs at this sorry, sterile juncture in our history, not more well-schooled zombies on whose backs the few can ride?

Did we ever have a society like that? Of course we did. Take yourself back to the days of Ben Franklin's Philadelphia, where the crackling energy of limitless possibility was everywhere, in a society where ages were mixed together promiscuously, where anyone could take a turn when they felt up to it, where possibilities popped like firecrackers. Boston was another example of this — research the unbelievable trade of ice to India as just one specimen of what is possible when imagination — and youth — go unregulated. Pittsburgh is another good place to look. Study the career of the ridiculous little Scottish bobbin-boy, Andrew Carnegie, who dropped out of elementary school at age 7 with an accent so thick everyone made fun of him. Follow his path, step by step, to Mrs. Botta's salon in Greenwich Village, where revolutions in Italy, Hungary and Cuba were being cooked up and financed, and then on to his wealth and sinister influence on a once relatively free society. The evidence is overwhelming what a hideous transformation has been made to occur, partly through schooling. But you must *work* to understand and gain courage to defeat the plan — nobody can do it for you.

Four More School Failures

Hemingway, the school dropout, once said all modern American literature can be traced back to Mark Twain, born in Missouri in 1835, in terrible health for the first ten years of his life. Comedians such as Eddie Murphy, Jon Stewart, and Stephen Colbert are descended from Twain, whose profound insight — that "irreverence, not schooling" is the creator of liberty — is a mark of his brilliance. Twain named and anatomized the "gilded age" for that period of boundless greed which followed Union victory in the Civil War, and from whose Machiavellianism the wretched institution of modern forced schooling began.

Mark Twain dropped out of school after fifth grade and went to work for a newspaper. He was 13, the year was 1848. In 2008 as I speak and write, that sort of blank-check possibility has been foreclosed on for the young, to please the managers of things.

Segue now to Robert Kiyosaki, a fourth-generation Japanese American, born in Hawaii in 1946. At school, according to his own report, "the only courses I excelled in were football and lunch. Most people didn't think I'd amount to anything." At 22, Kiyosaki was third mate on a tanker going to Tahiti. Shortly after, he joined the Marines for six years and after discharge, started his first business, which failed. He lost everything, including his marriage.

But at 37 his first break came when he studied with Buckminster Fuller, the Harvard dropout, who showed Robert that the deepest learning arises from mistakes and failure. Kiyosaki says today that if he ever builds a brand new educational system he will "build it around making mistakes." That's almost the operational definition of open-source education, sharpening your own personal feedback loops through experience and mistakes.

From penniless bankrupt to wealthy man took Robert eight years. You've heard of him as author of *Rich Dad, Poor Dad,* a kind of teacher's masterpiece. Many consider him one of the finest teachers alive in the world today.

Kindness Over Profit

John Mackey, founder of the Whole Foods Market chain, and Kip Tindell, founder of The Container Store chain, roomed together in Austin, where they played poker (a lot) while trying (not very hard) to get through the University of Texas. Both eventually dropped out, Mackey to open a health food store, Tindell to honor his obsession, which was to help people organize their messy lives.

In time, Mackey's health food store became Whole Foods Market, the nation's leading natural food emporium; and Tindell's organizational dream turned into The Container Store, a unique national chain without any clear competition. Both men found a way to add value to the world around them after they dropped out. They took their turn when the time was right; who knows whether their grand successes would have happened had they waited for a degree, or two, or three.

Mackey and Tindell had worked out a common philosophy as young men back in Austin, a radical philosophy which no business school in America would dream of teaching — that the primary purpose of business is not to make money for owners and shareholders, but to satisfy customers. Such a point of view would be unfathomable to the B-school crowd everywhere, though oddly enough, the Adam Smith who wrote *Theory of Moral Sentiments* would understand it without difficulty. Smith regarded the insatiable desire to make a lot of money as a mental disease. As do I.

Treating customers as if they matter more than profit should sound tantalizingly familiar to you, if you've been paying attention. It's an echo of Paul's directive that loving your neighbor (and your enemies) is the only way to win at life. The educated spirit can see through the illusions of winning as only dark phantasms, thoroughly conditioned in school by constant petty competitions and superiority/inferiority symbolisms. Education (not schooling) teaches what really matters, that adding value to others is the only way to add value to yourself. If you aren't useful you must be useless — and nobody wants that.

The real wealth society throws away when it allows crazy social and political leadership to stigmatize and even commodify school dropouts, and those without college degrees, is incalculable. For every John and Kip, Ingvar, Edison, Danica, or Lew Wasserman who survives the prejudice, many more are crushed by it and just give up.

The most reckless failure of our modern American nation is how we waste people in the interest of keeping systems efficient. Systems won't protect us in the time of the sweat bath we've entered; systems can't heal the diseased economy which systems-thinkers have built — only sovereign human spirits intact can do that, the kind which can't be fashioned in factory schools.

We used to make steel, now we make bubbles — with the strangest economic bubble of them all being the swollen and cancerous school bubble, early childhood to graduate college, a utopian growth which costs much more than any dividends it yields. It breaks families, intellects, characters. It visits incompetence on tens of millions. It's a black hole of negative energy draining vitality from national life. Just losing the young from the everyday world had pernicious effects, cumulative ones. We lost our libertarian momentum in the wall-to-wall conformity well-regulated corporate life demands; we lost our unity, our cohesion, in the face of the many divisions and disconnections confinement schooling requires.

After the post-WWII boom years of the 1950s, school — one-time servant of corporate America — morphed into the largest corporation of all. It became the master corporation bleeding resources from the productive economy in a parasitic relationship which had no governor on its growth, just as cancer cells have no limits until the host dies.

We used to make steel, now we make bubbles — vast synthetic rushes of enthusiasm for real estate, high tech, health care, prison construction, whatever the schooled public, lacking ability to think for itself, can be stampeded into clamoring for, but the weirdest bubble of them all is the school bubble — kindergarten through graduate college — which robs the economy of the material resources and, more important, the fresh vision needed to move our sick society in a new direction.

By the beginning of the 21st century, the lion's share of revenue at American automakers came not from cars but from sophisticated games with money. As this enthusiasm spread from the Harvard Business School (and other sources) into the corporate world in general, gigantic enterprises like Enron and Worldcom vanished in a matter of months, carrying down with them the life savings of tens of thousands of employees and hundreds of thousands, or millions, of stockholders. The entire corporate edifice showed signs of old age, albeit brought periodically back to life with a new bubble. As I began to write this book in early 2008, Bear Stearns — America's fifth-largest investment bank — lost virtually all its value in a period of months by gambling in unsound mortgages, and since then Lehman Brothers, America's fourth largest investment bank, has joined it in collapse.

Signs that the culture was a body oozing life were everywhere, and everywhere denied by the managers of schooling (and everything else): We could no longer harvest our own food, but depended upon illegal immigration to do that; the economic base of our medical care industry was shaken at its foundations by massive defections of clientele for surgery, dental care, and medicines — which crossed the northern and southern border, or went to Asia to be cared for. Our armies, rich with machinery, but short on leadership, depended increasingly upon the poorest Americans to do the dying in a lengthening string of foreign wars best seen not as wars at all, but only as more bubbles.

In the face of such forbidding omens, with the future promising more of the same, the school scene — like the salt-grinding little machine in the fable — continued to grind out incomplete men and women as it had always done. At the exact historical moment which was calling for a renewed commitment to imagination, courage, self-reliance, resourcefulness and other early American virtues, the school mill labored to turn out young people without these attributes.

St. Paul and the Rulebook Dragon

> The Dutch city of Drachten did away with traffic signs, parking meters, and even parking spaces as part of a program called "verkeersbordvrij." The results have been pleasantly shocking: Traffic safety has improved dramatically. Under circumstances where they are drawn into leadership roles, people take it upon themselves to look out for their own and others' best interest, even in the absence of rules and enforcement.
>
> — paraphrased from Jonathan Zittrain,
> *The Future of the Internet*, pp 127–128

St. Paul's New Testament letters to the congregations (which later coalesced into the Christian movement) have something to say to us all about what needs changing in the way we school. For Paul, excessive regulation ruins the quality of life and corrupts leadership by requiring bureaucrats to enforce the rules, and more officials to regulate those officials. *Ad infinitum.*

In many different words, Paul repeats over and over that the new congregations won't find salvation by following the old rules. Eliminate the religious background for a minute and what Paul faced was the school problem of our own day — the conflict between interest groups whose income and status derives from keeping things as they are, and an insurgency whose needs have been neglected by the entrenched management and which demands profound change.

Translated into contemporary idiom, Paul says make up the rules as you go along to fit individual cases. As long as the root principle of love is honored, then things will work out.

The political establishment of Paul's day was the ancient Israel of the *Mishnah,* a stupendous collection of rules for even the most obscure circumstances like the height from which someone should pour water on a manure pile. Like modern bureaucratic schooling, there can be little adaptation to particular cases, the system is wedded to certainty. Find a thief? Cut off his nose! Find an adultress? Stone her to death! When in doubt, don't think — follow the rules.

The new insurgency travelled a different road. If someone steals your coat, give him your cloak, too; if someone strikes your left cheek, turn the right one to be struck, too. Unto this last: pay workmen who labor half a day the same wage as those who labor a whole day.

Rule book people find these pronouncements maddening, incomprehensible. Our forced schooling has brought back the rule-choked social environment of Paul's day, and our surveillance society has provided the technology to punish deviants which Paul's lacked. Through the three-headed rule monster of school and college, corporations, and government, American society has been radically de-individualized, one in every five American jobs is some form of oversight over the behavior of others.

It is six times more likely you will end up in jail in the United States than it is in Communist China (which now possesses the ability to ruin America economically by cashing in its loan to us). Six times more likely to rot in jail here than in China. All by itself that fact should cause you to re-evaluate the road that leadership — of all our political parties and corporations — has committed us to walking. It is the schools which keep us on that road.

The insurgency of 21st century America, still disorganized but daily becoming less so, has made its presence felt through the explosive growth of homeschooling, through the Internet, and through various novel areas of crime. Identity theft, a rarity throughout history, has become an unstoppable epidemic; huge commercial operations in film and music are seriously jeopardized by technologies which return control to the individual. The security of banks, government installations, and much more — like patents and copyrights — is under serious siege.

Formulas for powerful weapons like the TATP bomb which paralyzed London subways a few years ago, compounded from six pounds of peroxide, paint remover, and drain cleaner in the ratio of 3/3/1, stabilized with sawdust, and stuffed into a strong steel container to be detonated by a cell phone are circulating widely across the planet. Those materials cost less than $100 and are available in every hardware store on Earth.

Our reckless military operations in Vietnam, Iraq, and Afganistan, have violated central precepts of warfare set down by Von Clausewitz — a superior technology doesn't promiscuously attack its victims, it *threatens*. To commit a major attack is to expose your technology to scrutiny, which holds two dangers: first, that expensive machinery is badly overmatched against an insurgency trained in guerrilla tactics, and second, that the enemy will gradually upgrade his own technology by studying your tactics and stealing your weapons. What America has to show for 50 years of continuous warfare against weak, stone-age opponents, is this: besides crippling our future with a reckless expenditure of capital on products which produce nothing, like weaponry, and destroy themselves in use, we have notified every corner of the world that our overwhelming military isn't overwhelming at all and can be beaten by ordinary people of courage, with primitive military hardware, who refuse to be intimidated.

Surely I can't be the only one to notice that Sunnis and Shiites and Taliban have reasons to risk their lives, (reasons known to everyone in the population including their fighters), and we do not. Our reasons to fight are locked up in secret meetings and memos known to a small fraction of the population — the same fraction which, not surprisingly, once upon a time gave us forced institutional schooling.

The Time of the Sweat Bath

The day of the expert, and of an elite created by rationing information and using the power of government to load the dice, has reached a crisis point I don't think it can deal with. Existing contracts between ourselves and the young don't work anymore. By supporting school-imposed order, however innocently, parents make enemies of their own children, sometimes lifelong enemies. Rimbaud, the young French poet, saw prophetically into the future this modern order of secular industrial values was creating. Over a hundred years ago, he wrote this, which fits our time better than his:

> This is the time of the sweat bath, of oceans boiling over, of underground explosions, of the planet whirled away, of exterminations sure to follow.

In a time of the sweat bath, would you prefer as allies "A" students with high SATs, or a walkabout like Richard Branson? A valedictorian or a surf bum like Craig Venter? Formulaic schooling is worthless to common citizens, even destructive. It's only useful to policymakers and managers. It must be killed, not modified. Attempts to tinker with its ruthless algorithms prolongs our society's agony and makes the situation worse. Reach into the public bazaar for guidance, not to old-fashioned cathedral builders who created the mess we're in (and will recreate eternally if given the chance). Yes, it will take courage, and no, I don't expect leadership of either American poltical party to find it. But *you* can.

Professionalism functions as a hardening of the social arteries. Its limited utility comes at far too high a price, a price which must be charged against the account of what really matters: good health, good relationships, and good, satisfying work.

As I wrote this originally, I was listening to National Public Radio interviewing a senior from Virginia Tech, the scene of the worst massacre so far in American school history. Asked what made her happy about returning to class, without hesitation she announced that it was being able, finally, to take her year-end exams. The interviewer was puzzled, and asked "why that?" She needed no time to reply. "Why, to see if I learned anything, of course." Here was the perfect product of the school factory — a young woman who would never be a problem for any important special interest. Or of any use to the rest of us when trouble comes.

Walkabout: Monongahela

I never walked through London as a four-year-old boy, but back in the early 1940s during World War II, I walked through the industrial river town of Monongahela, Pennsylvania several times a week at night, walked miles and miles with my mother, Bootie, and my sister Joanie. We walked only at night so nobody my mother had once known would notice her and her children peering into the lighted windows of homes she had once frequented as a guest. We were living in her hometown, unseen, because she was embarrassed at the failure of her marriage.

We were like anthropologists doing field studies, sister and I, studying our mother in different circumstances than we usually saw her: dusting, doing laundry, washing dishes. And mother was seeing her own early self through a different filter, too. Whatever our motives for repeating the same long route through the darkened hill streets over and over, I can't remember, but I know I never tired of it. We were all happy as pigs in the moon that is young once only — though usually in pocket no more than a nickel with which to buy one candy bar which we broke into three shares.

Those walks were transcendental experiences of a very high order; even at an age when many experiences seemed transcendental, they were outstanding. As an old man, I now see they were easily the richest family experience I was ever to have. And my greatest educational adventure, too, just as Branson's walk was his.

We took the last walk together around 1947. Beginning seven years later and continuing for years afterward, I attended five colleges, two of them Ivy League, but my degree schooling proved to be a waste of time where intellectual development was concerned. I can't seem to recall a single thing I learned at those famous universities, Cornell and Columbia; not a single class, not a single teacher. Yet I remember everything about those walks, down to the tiniest details.

Each excursion covered roughly five miles. We wove in and out of the darkened hill streets, reaching zones of settlement I was only dimly aware existed. I still hear our footsteps crunching the fall leaves or the winter snow, or sloshing through the spring rains. I can hear our hushed whispers. Every house had a story, and mother knew all of them. Many had a symbol in the front window telling the world that some man inside had gone away off to the wars. In some windows there was a special symbol — I seem to remember it was a gold star like they used to give to the best schoolchildren for exceptional work — a symbol which declared the man had died in service to the rest of us.

The presence of death on our walks added something wonderfully deep and profound to the rambles, a sadness reminding me at the corners of consciousness that someday my mother would be dead, too, and my sister, and myself.

From time to time mother would reminisce what a particular soldier or sailor, once her schoolmate, had been like as a living boy. For a little fellow this was like being confronted with ghosts. It was stunning drama. How dull those walks, and those deaths, made all my toys. In the face of a dramatic reality that ennobled, even the most ordinary toys were less than insignificant; they were humiliating by contrast, unspeakably childish. Real stories help a boy grow up; toys beyond a point reached in early childhood retard the hard road to maturity.

I learned more about mother and sister from those walks than I could fully comprehend back then; today I realize that the personal information gathered incidentally as we walked was the most important data I was ever to have about who we Gattos and Zimmers really were. The walks were open-source learning of the highest order. I'd gladly trade Cornell and Columbia for more of them.

Sixty-five years have passed since the last walk. Reflecting on what I learned that way without effort tells me the most powerful educations are always put together open-source. They can't be achieved from somebody else's idea of which controlled inputs under which artificial conditions produce the best outputs. The analogy of education with laboratory science is a game for fools, learned fools who have damaged lives beyond numbering, ruined the promise of America, and have brought us face-to-face with a bleak future unless the expansion of the schooling bubble can be reversed.

The rigid stupidities of forced schooling, its linear logics, its bell curves, its buzzers and tests and multiple humiliations, its resort to magical spells, fills me with rage these days as an old man. Real education can only begin out of a foundation of self-awareness. Know the truth of yourself or you are nothing but a pathetic human resource. Your life will have missed its point.

These are my reflections on Richard Branson's walkabout and my own, and on the crime schooling commits daily by turning its back on open-source learning.

In 2007, an indomitable Australian woman, Eleanor Sparks, and her friends, conceived, organized, and staged that continent's first national homeschool convention. It was staged, serially, in ten major cities coast to coast, including Hobart, Tasmania. "Walkabout: London" was the keynote speech for that convention.

3

Fat Stanley and the Lancaster Amish

I Don't Take Criticism Well

Separate schooling and education into compartments, and useful distinctions jump out at you: schooling is a matter of habit and attitude training. It takes place from the outside in. Education is a matter of self-mastery, first; then self-enlargement, even self-transcendence — as all possibilities of the human spirit open themselves into zones for exploration and understanding. There are points where the two conditions inform one another, but in schooling, somebody else's agenda is always uppermost. This mind control aspect is what makes it so unpleasant, even pornographic to some, although not to the lost souls already broken to the game of pleasing others. You can easily compensate for a lack of schooling — the human record is full of stories of those who have done so in the past and those who continue to do so in the present — but without education you will stumble through life, a sitting duck for exploitation and failure, no matter how much money you make.

Mary Shelley wrote the story of Frankenstein at the age of 18, nearly 200 years ago. Today, it's studied in college courses as a profound work of literature. That famous Stratford nobody, William Shakespeare, had little seat time in a classroom, and owned no books, apparently, yet four centuries after his death he remains an icon of global civilization. The list is a long one. Large accomplishments; little schooling. It's quite rare for an inventive person in any field to trace success to school training. Education must be largely self-initiated, a tapestry woven out of broad experience, constant introspection, ability to concentrate on one's purpose in spite of distractions, a combination of curiosity, patience, and intense watchfulness, and it requires substantial trial and error risk-taking, along with a considerable ability to take feedback from the environment — to learn from mistakes. I once heard someone in my own family, who I once loved very much, say, "I don't take criticism well," as if it were a boast, and I knew at that instant there was no way at all for her to grow in mind or character with that self-destructive attitude.

Let me tell you a little about fat Stanley, whose path crossed mine when he was thirteen. Stanley only came to class one or two days a month, and I knew that sooner or later he would be caught in the truancy net and prosecuted. I liked Stanley, not least because he never whined when other kids bothered him because he was fat — he simply punched them so hard in the head nobody ever bothered Stanley a second time. I hoped to spare him the grim experience of becoming a social service case. So I asked him one day what he did on all those absences? What he said changed my life. I never saw school the same way after Stanley spoke.

It seems Stanley had five aunts and uncles, all in business for themselves before the age of 21. His aim was to follow in their footsteps. Even at 13, he had been made aware of time's winged chariot hurrying near, that he had only eight years to make the miracle of an independent livelihood. One of the relatives was a florist, one a builder of unfinished furniture, one a deli owner, one had a little restaurant, one owned a delivery service. Stanley cut school to work without pay for each of these relatives, bartering labor in exchange for learning the businesses — and a whole lot more — working in the company of men and women who cared for him much more than any professional stranger would have.

It was a better educational package than whatever he missed cutting school, hands down. As he put it to me, man to man: "This way I get a chance to see how the different businesses work. You tell me what books I have to read and I'll read them. But I don't have time to waste in school unless I want to end up like you — working for somebody else." When I heard that, I couldn't keep him locked up in good conscience. Besides, his mother agreed with Stanley. So I began to cover for him, logging him present when he was making floral bouquets or building furniture. None of his other teachers ever asked; I think they were glad to be rid of him. To illustrate the powerful energies at work under his fat, deceptively cheerful exterior, Stanley crossed his "t"s with a pointed spear formation, not a simple line. Right then and there I adopted his "t" cross as my own, to remind me what I learned from a truant that day.

A big secret of bulk-process schooling is that it doesn't teach the way children learn; a bigger secret is that it isn't supposed to teach self-direction at all. Stanley-style is *verboten*. School is about learning to wait your turn, however long it takes to come, *if ever*. And how to submit with a show of enthusiasm to the judgment of strangers, even if they are wrong; even if your enthusiasm is phony.

School is the first impression we get of organized society and its relentless need to rank everyone on a scale of winners and losers; like most first impressions, the real things school teaches about your place in the social order last a lifetime for most of us.

Work in classrooms isn't important work. It fails to speak to real needs pressing on the young. It doesn't answer burning questions which day-to-day experience forces upon young minds. Problems encountered outside school walls are treated as peripheral when in truth they are always central. The net effect of making work abstract —

"subject"-centered — external to individual longings, fears, experiences, and questions, is to render students of this enforced irrelevance listless and indifferent.

The causes of sluggishness in the young have been well understood for a long time. I'm tempted to say forever. Growth and self-mastery are reserved for those who vigorously self-direct, like Stanley: planning, doing, creating, reflecting, freely associating, taking chances, punching the lights out on your tormentors. But this is precisely the agenda school is set up to prevent. Think of school as a conditioning laboratory, drilling naturally unique, one-of-a-kind individuals to respond as a mass, to accept continual ennui, envy and limited competence as only natural parts of the human condition. The official economy we have constructed demands constantly renewed supplies of leveled, spiritless, passive, anxious, friendless, family-less people who can be scrapped and replaced endlessly, and who will perform at maximum efficiency until their own time comes to be scrap; people who think the difference between Coke and Pepsi, or round hamburgers versus square ones, are subjects worthy of argument.

As I wrote those words in February of 2008, I had just finished listening to a commercial for high-style telephones on TV. It made fun of the unfortunate fools whose telephone styling was "soooo yesterday," as a pretty girl put it in the advertisement. It had never before occurred to me that among various inescapable worries like cancer, homelessness, unemployment, blindness, aging, poverty, crippling accidents and the like, there might actually be people so shallow the look of their telephone was an item of concern. Try to picture the "A" student who came up with that idea, and pray for his contemptible soul.

The Old Order Amish

I tried to imagine the Lancaster Amish, or any of the Old Order Amish scattered around the world, worrying whether their telephones were in fashion. The small business, small farm economy of the Amish requires different qualities from the oncoming generations than we do: they ask for broad competence and a spirit of self-reliance, for dependability, honesty, neighborliness, compassion, piety, and commitment to the common good. Were we to adopt Amish values wholesale, our economy would nosedive.

As our economy has been shaped by its architects, it relies upon encouraging frenzy for novelty, for fashion in more than clothing, all the way to telephones. It's an attitude which induces nonstop consumption in a heady atmosphere of "out with the old, in with the new;" to escape from shame, an addiction to the spirit of the Cole Porter song, *Anything Goes*. That's the job the incessant bells perform in our schools: they teach a Monty Pythonesque relief at escape from responsibility, as they say in bell language, "And now for something completely different." Of course, you have to have deep experience with shame to fear it. But schools are an advanced workshop in that, too. The first day I taught, an old-timer told me how to control my classes. "Humiliation," she said. "That's the only thing they fear. Shame them. Encourage other kids to shame them, too."

One famous insider of modern schooling back in the post-WWI days (when the model was hardening) called government schooling "the perfect organization of the hive." That was H. H. Goddard, chairman of psychology at Princeton. Goddard believed standardized test scores used as a signal for privileged treatment would cause the lower classes to come face to face with their own biological inferiority. It would be like wearing a public dunce cap. Exactly the function "special education" delivers today. The pain of endless daily humiliation would discourage reproduction among the inferior, Goddard thought. Charles Darwin had implied this gently, but his first cousin, Francis Galton, had virtually demanded it of responsible politicians on both sides of the Atlantic in his own writings.

In 1930, the Department of Superintendence of the National Education Association, a group then basking in reflected glory from the lessons of schooling in the new Soviet Union, declared the main purpose of schooling should be "effective use of capital," that valuable stuff through which "our unprecedented wealth-producing power has been gained." Now how do you suppose *that* idea got into circulation among the folks at a presumably left-wing organization? Talk about a house of mirrors! For the curious, you might want to buy Anthony Sutton's *Wall Street and the Rise of the Soviet Union.*

Think for a second how "capital" can become "more effective." Surely it happens when the stuff capital allows to be produced is actually *purchased* by eager consumers, and when projects financed by capital receive little public resistance. Capital operates most efficiently in climates without public opposition, where critical thinking among ordinary people is in a primitive state, so the public becomes an inept opponent. And is it so difficult to conceive of a plan which could be managed through the very institution — schooling — charged with development of the intellect? It isn't by accident the symbol of Fabian socialism is a wolf in sheep's clothing, or that Fabians were from the comfortable classes of England, not from its marginalized dregs (as was often true of revolutionary socialists). This is a matter of some significance, though never held up to scrutiny in schoolbook histories. Where industrial management was content to kill the masses with brutal treatment, Fabians, led by Beatrice Webb, aimed to kill them with kindness. Hence we got the Welfare State. But whatever the methods, aims were identical.

If school is to serve capital, then it must be a production line where children as raw material are shaped and fashioned like nails. To make capital more efficient would require capital accumulations be concentrated into fewer hands, not spread so widely among the populace. Even that the middle-class basis of American society give way a little, too. Or eventually, give way a lot.

Sixty-six years after this weirdly indiscreet slip by the NEA's Department of Superintendence, Johns Hopkins University Press, in 1996, published a book, *Fat and Mean,* with surprising news about our by now well-schooled society. The book reported that while the American economy had grown massively through the 1960s, real spendable working-class wages *hadn't grown at all for 30 years.* During the booms of the 1980s and 1990s, purchasing power had risen steeply for 20 percent of the population, but it actually declined for all the rest by 13 percent. After inflation was factored in, purchasing power of a working couple in 1995 was only 8 percent greater than for a *single* working man in 1905.

The steep decline in common prosperity over 90 years of intense forced schooling drove both parents from the home to work, depositing their children in the management systems of daycare and extended schooling. Despite a century-long harangue that schooling is the cure for unevenly spread wealth, exactly the reverse occurred. Wealth was 250 percent more concentrated at century's end than at its beginnings.

The Old Order Amish took a different road. Today a group of about 150,000 people — quite prosperous although virtually unschooled — this group held together by religion and common culture came to the US with little more than the clothes on their backs. In his book *Amish Enterprise*, published in 1995, author Donald Kraybill, a specialist in Amish life and a Johns Hopkins University academic, said the Amish

> challenge a lot of conventional assumptions about what it takes to enter business. They don't have high school educations; they don't have specialized training; they don't use computers; they don't use electricity or automobiles; they don't have training in how to create a marketing plan. But the resources they transfer over from the farm are: an entrepreneurial spirit; a willingness to take risks; innovativeness; a strong work ethic; a cheap family labor pool; and high standards of craftsmanship. They don't want their shops and industries to get large. This spreads entrepreneurship widely across the whole settlement.

More. The Amish are legendary good neighbors, first to volunteer in times of need in the larger non-Amish community. They open their farms to ghetto children and frequently rear handicapped children from the non-Amish world whom nobody else wants. They farm so well and so profitably without using chemical fertilizers or pesticides, without tractors and other complex machinery, that Canada, Russia, France, Mexico and Uruguay have hired them to help raise agricultural productivity outside the United States.

In *Yoder v. Wisconsin* (1976), the Amish did battle with the government of Wisconsin to preserve their way of doing things against bureaucratic assault. And although the decision looks like a compromise in which both parties won a little, a closer look will leave no doubt of which was the real winner.

Sick of Amish rejection of its schools, Wisconsin sought to compel Amish compliance with its secular school laws through its police power. The Amish resisted on these grounds: they said government schooling was built on the principle of the mechanical milk separator. It whirled the young mind about until both the social structure of the Amish community, and the structure of private family life, were fragmented beyond repair. Schooling demanded separation of people from daily life, it divided the world into disciplines, courses, classes, grades and teachers who would remain strangers to the children in all but name. Even religion, separated from family and daily life, was just another subject for critical analysis and testing.

And the constant competition was destructive, leaving a multitude of losers, humiliated and self-hating, a far cry from the universal commitment Amish community life requires. The Amish wanted no part of these things. As a part of any compromise with Wisconsin, community leaders demanded the following:

1. Schools within walking distance of home.
2. No school to be so large that pupils had to be sorted into different compartments and assigned different teachers every year.
3. The school year would be no longer than eight months.
4. Important decisions would be under parental control, not that of bureaucrats.
5. Teachers hired were to be knowledgeable in, and sympathetic to, Amish values and rural ways.

6. Children were to be taught that wisdom and academic knowledge were two different things.
7. Every student would have practical internships and apprenticeships supervised by parents.

What can be learned from Stanley and the Amish? One thing, to discard any belief that the concept of mass man actually describes something real. We need to realize what our fingerprints and our intuition actually proclaimed long before DNA: no two people are alike, all "averages" are lies, and nobody can be accurately contained by numbers and graphs. The use of these against those too weak to resist is the Bed of Procrustes, brought into modern life. We need to abandon the notion — and punish those who retain it — that ordinary people are too stupid, irresponsible, and childish to look out for themselves. We need to honor our founding documents and founding ideas, to accept that each one of us has the right to live as he or she deems wise, and if the way chosen would mean disaster for global corporations — as the way of the Amish and the Stanleys among us surely would — then that decision must be honored still.

4

David Sarnoff's Classroom

A Letter to My Assistant Principal

Dear Murray,

I enjoyed our talk last Friday about the hidden machinery in School District Three, Manhattan. You surprised me with your candor. I hope we can build on that to exchange some ideas (discreetly of course), which might prove of mutual benefit. I know official pedagogy doesn't forgive those who expose its secrets, so in light of the fact you told me you expect to work here "forever," in what follows I've exercised some discretion in the event this falls into hostile hands. I have left my own presence intact, you'll notice. In the first place I have no intention of working here forever, and in the second place I grew up in the Monongahela Valley near Pittsburgh around the time of WWII, and I was taught by that Scots-Irish place (even in its schools), to welcome a fight with rotters, scoundrels and low-lifes, all which labels fit our mutual employers.

Recently I walked through the Harvard campus in Cambridge, just for the fun of it, and on that ramble I spotted a brochure pinned to a bulletin board in one of the buildings, containing advice for students planning a career in the new international economy which it predicted was at hand. First, the brochure gave warning that academic classwork and professional credentials would count for less in the future, and a track record of accomplishment which suggested competency would count for more. This seemed a way to put a bell around the neck of grade point averages and test rankings, fingering them for the frauds they are, albeit in the time-honored elliptical manner of charlatans everywhere. That caught my interest, so I read on.

The brochure identified nine qualities its author felt were essential for successful adaptation to the evolving world of work, so I'm asking you, Murray, to temporarily put aside your customary apologia for District Three's shameless schools and let me know how many of the nine you can honestly say are the priorities of the wealthy school district we work for on the Upper Westside of Manhattan:

1. The ability to ask hard questions of data, whether from textbooks, authorities, or other "expert" sources. In other words, do we teach dialectics?
2. The ability to define problems independently, to avoid slavish dependence on official definitions.
3. The ability to scan masses of irrelevant information and to quickly extract from the sludge whatever is useful.
4. The ability to conceptualize.
5. The ability to reorganize information into new patterns which enable a different perspective than the customary.
6. The possession of a mind fluent in moving among different modes of thought: deductive, inductive, heuristic, intuitive, et al.
7. Facility in collaboration with a partner, or in teams.
8. Skill in the discussion of issues, problems or techniques.
9. Skill in rhetoric. Convincing others your course is correct.

Now, from where I sit, and I've been sitting in District Three for nearly three decades, we don't teach any of these as a matter of policy. And for good reason. Students so trained would destroy the structure of familiar schooling and all the comfortable hierarchies some of us depend on.

Just think for a second about the transmission of competencies. Our school population is drawn largely from families of the working poor, but we've abandoned shop and cooking programs, interscholastic athletics, school socials, art and music. Not only can't our kids read, write, or count very well; now they can't drive a nail, plane a board, use a saw, turn a screwdriver, boil an egg, or find ways to amuse themselves and stay healthy. In a few classrooms, very few, teachers know how to train the young in powers; but actually *doing* this has to be accomplished as a kind of sabotage because it would never be authorized by authority. Every deviation from standardized protocol has to be signed off on multiple times, making it almost impossible to teach correctly, to adapt to particular people, conditions, and opportunities.

Now, for contrast, think of David Sarnoff's school — the streets. Sarnoff, as head of RCA, has been a major power in the twentieth century, yet his early years were spent in a *shtetl* in Russia without schooling. Promptly upon arrival in New York City with his family, his father dropped dead — leaving David at age nine to be family breadwinner. In five short months he could read English well enough to read the daily newspapers, and could speak it well enough to earn the family living as a newsboy — half a cent for every paper sold. Was it English classes in school that inspired such facility, do you think?

Five months to operational fluency. No school. What do you make of that, Murray? At fourteen Sarnoff had his own newsstand. Without time for a high school diploma, little David read the daily papers as his texts. One day he saw an ad for an office boy at Marconi Wireless. He hurried over to the company without an appointment, barged into the office of the president unannounced, and asked for the job. Five hundred boys in line to be interviewed, but it was David who was hired on the spot. There's a lesson there, Murray. I wish our school could teach it. Waiting your turn is often the worst way to get what you want.

After a year as an office boy, Sarnoff taught himself telegraphy just as Andy Carnegie had done in Pittsburgh at an even younger age. When Marconi Wireless was swallowed up by the Radio Corporation of America, he was on the cutting edge of the technology it needed, thanks to self-teaching. Twenty-three years later, age 39, he was president of the company.

How could that happen without money, family connections, a high school diploma, or a college degree?! Sounds like a soap opera or an Alger story. Murray, don't dare say "those were simpler times" like a parrot repeating something it heard; those were far more complicated times than this barren epoch we enjoy, stripped of human meaning by the corporatizing of everything. At age nine, Sarnoff self-taught himself into a job; at 14 into a business; at 39, into the presidency of a powerful, tech-driven corporation.

He was able to move so rapidly also because he got a chance to think about serious matters before his eighth birthday, to live a significant life before he was ten. He got a chance to add value to his family and community before he was 15, and a chance to follow his own instincts and ambitions ever after. What school do you know these days that would allow that? If we followed the same path, school would cease to be the jobs-project it really is.

You can't self-teach without inner strength and a measure of gravity, without opportunities to be alone, to have broad experience with people and great challenges. Most of us who presume to judge schools are fooled by rituals of disciplined behavior, pretty hall displays, and test scores. If we knew what to look for, we'd be horrified and angry at the empty destinies this waste of precious time arranges for us.

The Mask of School Reform

I was recently a visitor to a famous alternative public school in East Harlem which received truckloads of compliments over the past few years. It was founded and run by a famous woman, Debbie Meier, a lady with a reputation for plain talk and straight shooting. I had known Mrs. Meier very slightly for about a decade before I saw her school, and I have no hesitation saying she deserved all the nice things said about her: she was smart as a whip, tough as nails, and generous to a fault.

But looking at the school from inside for a few hours it was impossible not to see how far it fell short of standards of excellence which aren't very hard to achieve — and which once were common to schools in the steel-working Monongahela Valley where I grew up. Right near the surface I could see this famous East Harlem school was seriously hobbled by familiar constraints, many self-imposed by habit, by custom, by lack of imagination, and by the school district, too, I would imagine. The famous negative litany: You can't do this; you can't do that; time to move to something different; you better take the upcoming test seriously, etc., was alive and well at the famous school.

My guess is none of this was Debbie's doing, but realistically she had to function inside a mature bureaucracy, one very conscious just how far deviation could be allowed before top management would be called on the carpet and punished.

The most suffocating of the constraints are generated from traditional Calvinistic roots: Mistrust of children, mistrust of teachers, a reluctance to face that adolescence is a junk word, fear of looking bad, fear of scoring poorly on standardized tests, and suppression of imagination — voluntary suppression — which the collective teaching staff imposes on those of its colleagues who haven't yet lost their talent.

For weeks after that visit I felt awful. Debbie's school was clearly a better place for kids than the schools of District Three, and yet David Sarnoff wouldn't have wasted his time there, nor would the place have had anything real to offer Mr. Sarnoff. What hit me hardest was the community service program at Central Park East — community service was a requirement of attendance, and one I used extensively in my own teaching practice. It had produced stunning benefits in all areas of curriculum for me, I was a believer.

And yet at this famous school — enrolling students older than David Farragut was when he took over command of a warship; older than Washington was when he learned trigonometry, surveying, naval architecture and military science — at this famous school students were assigned to community service for two hours a week. Two hours a week. Who in their right mind would *want* a teenager to drop in for two hours a week, with all the bookkeeping, training, oversight, and hassle that would require? It was a way of fatally trivializing the service ideal, turning it into superficial drudgery for all concerned.

The Commissioner's Report

Once a principal in the richest secondary school in District Three — you'll know the one I mean, Murray — asked me privately if I could help him set up a program to teach critical thinking. Of course, I replied, but if we do it right your school will become unmanageable. Why would kids taught to think critically and express themselves effectively put up with the nonsense you force down their throats? That was the end of our interview and his critical thinking project.

Murray, you're the only individual who ever willingly spoke to me about the apparatus of pedagogy, in all 26 years I've been in the business. The only one. In the thousands of hours I've spent in teachers' rooms and teachers' meetings, not a single soul besides yourself was open to discussing anything profound about our notions of pedagogy, nothing that could get them in trouble. Surely that intellectual vacuum says something terrible about the business which has swallowed your life and my own.

My compliment is bait on the hook of my *next* question: At the end of 1988, our rich district was ranked statistically last by the State Commissioner of Education in a dull publication which looked like a telephone directory. You had to massage the numbers a long time to actually figure out what it was saying, but when I did, it seemed to be saying that we were the worst school district in New York State, 736th of 736, in certain key categories. But our section of the city is world famous, isn't it? We have great universities, famous research institutions, museums, centers for art, the best transportation system around...what gives?

You know what contempt I have for the instruments used to rank the student body, but in this one case I'm going to be inconsistent and cite them as a measure of school district failure. In third-grade math and reading, we rank dead last. We are only nine places off the bottom in fifth-grade writing, sixth-grade reading, math and social studies — and in seventh-grade honor math and honor biology.

Listen, friend; we can't be *last* or nearly *last* out of 736 school jurisdictions in so many metrics without being abysmal, not just bad. *Last* isn't an easy degree of failure to achieve; being last is a creative act. The Sarnoff family should thank its lucky stars District Three didn't get its hooks into David. This is the business you want to stay in "forever"? It boggles the mind. You ought to feel ashamed to take money for wasting the lives of these trapped children. I've gone to many school board meetings looking, like Diogenes, for one honest board member or administrator, one person who looked to be worried. But all I ever heard were waves of self-congratulation and a smug indifference to the suffering we were causing.

According to the Commissioner's Report, the average teacher in our schools has been there sixteen years, a sign of stability; yet the teacher turnover is an incredible 22% a year, almost the highest in New York State! What could account for such an anomaly? In some businesses turnover like that would cause a management shakeup. It damages morale; it causes a school to lose its memory. And yet... and yet, we have all those teachers who *stay*, too! Why? Let me tell you why.

A caste system has been created by school administrators, in combination with the teachers union. Certain teachers in each of our schools have been rewarded with good programs, good rooms, good kids in exchange for their loyalty and cooperation. The power to confer these privileges will be fatally enhanced if we ever get so-called "merit" pay (who would decide "merit" except feather-bedding administrators?). These favors are rewards for those who play ball, these privileges are bought by exploiting unfortunate fellow teachers, often the newest teachers who are dumped upon with impossible workloads, and quickly leave the business.

The situation I'm describing is universal and constitutes the poison pill in merit proposals. Merit would certainly NOT go to the meritorious — as a student, parent or citizen would define merit — but as a school administrator would. When 22% of the teachers don't survive more than a year, the caste system that corrupts our schools is partially to blame. Nobody ever bothers to ask the 100 to 150 teachers who leave each year why they left. That's because everyone already knows.

The Shadow Economy of Schools

Teachers with deals don't constitute the entirety of non-laboring labor in schools, there's been such an inflation of management, both visible and invisible, as to defy imagination. For instance, what do you make of this: the student/teacher ratio in our school district is listed in state accounts as 15:1, but everywhere the number of kids in a class is 30 or more: *Half of all teaching energy has been siphoned away* into administrative tasks in the shadow economy of front-office politics. No healthy enterprise can afford this degree of deceit. It's the teachers who *don't* get paid off with these non-teaching deals you should be worrying about. They become bitter and cynical. They find ways to get even, ways to cut back on their own production. You administrators have created a catastrophe by paying off your favorites with deals.

I can't escape the conclusion that we both are involved in a social engineering project whose mission is to weaken children's minds and give them bad characters — all concealed in the sanctimony we exude on parents' night. I heard one principal (a decent man in his own estimation, I'm sure), tell a large audience that the damage to these children had already been done before they came to him in seventh grade, and that his job was to relieve their pain and make them feel good in the here and now because their limited futures were already predetermined.

Can you believe it?! The shameless brass! I couldn't make that up. Isn't it the function of morphine or crack cocaine to stupefy pain? Given a choice between those substances and school *as an anodyne*, you'd have to be deranged to choose school.

Two district policies in particular have destroyed the capacity for sustained thought among our kids. The first was the political decision, cooked up at the Ford Foundation, as I recall, *not* to control outrageous classroom behavior on the grounds that frustration causes perpetrators to have low self-esteem. While this policy was being imposed (and afterwards), the *rhetoric* of decent behavior was maintained, as if nothing out of the ordinary were going on. Tell me, how was that any different from Big Brother announcing the chocolate ration was being raised, while it was being lowered? The degree of disrespect our nation has assigned its ordinary population wouldn't be possible unless somewhere in the command centers it hadn't been decided that common men and women should be stripped of any power to rebel. And that they could be lied to without compunction, because their dignity didn't count. Or their lives.

As these conditions for chaos were being imposed, a form of triage was constructed wherein a few of the "best" classes (on the liberal West Side, that means mostly white classes) were to be held to a traditional standard. As for the others, the mass of fairly well-behaved kids, was mixed with an infusion of violent, restless, disruptive students until only a primitive level of instruction was possible. In order to free school administrators from the tiresome function of helping to maintain order for the *lumpen proletariat,* classroom disruption was now deemed, system-wide, *a problem of bad teaching.* In other words, if you complained, or asked for help, you were treated with contempt and your job was in jeopardy. *Mirabile dictu!* The burden of discipline vanished as an administrative responsibility. And because reasonably patient children become angry at a teacher's ineffectiveness in maintaining order, many of the polite kids joined the disruptors, too. Does that surprise you, Murray? The cause and effect linkage, I mean.

Another destructive policy decision was the project to *recruit* disruptive children from other school districts, to conceal the shrinking enrollment in District Three — a student population decline caused by the evil reputation District Three acquired from its first policy! In 1984, after we fell to the lowest student enrollement of any district in New York City (10,000), 3,000 half-crazed children were recruited. It was like dumping the flotsam and jetsam of Cuban prisons on the United States in the boatlift days. This radical decision was taken without any consultation with parents at all, or with teachers who would be expected to manage these wild children. Incorporating them into hitherto calm classes, all hell broke loose, of course. How could it have been avoided? Principals began to lock their office doors. In short order, District Three plunged to the bottom of city statistical rankings. Then, to the bottom of the entire state! What a movie *that* would have made.

~

In 28 years of teaching, I've never seen an administrator attempt to raise the standard of what we expect from children, or what we expect from ourselves. We drown, however, in the rhetoric of high expectations which only those who wear tinfoil hats could take seriously. Changing superintendents makes no difference to the quality of schooling: some are fatter, some shriller, some black, some white, some Hispanic, some older or younger — but all dance to the same weird flute music from above. For decades I've watched a dreary parade of men and women make fine promises from the superintendent's office and every one eventually made some false move that angered their handlers and they were gone.

In all that time only one superintendent, a man who won his job thanks to a deal with my wife (the swing vote on the School Board at that time), agreed to assert independence from the cabal of influence peddlers and others who ran the district. Inside of a single year teacher morale soared — along with measures of accomplishment — and the district soared from the bottom of the city rankings to the mediocre center.

It was too much to bear. The fellow was fired for his cheek toward his betters, fired at a public meeting attended by all local politicians and political club leaders where he was denounced from the podium by a legendary West Side politician known to the media as "the conscience of the city council." You see, Murray, too much was at stake — not just money, but careers, patronage and ideological status — to allow any changes which would actually occur. It's the invisible stakeholders in schooling who would have to approve changes, and only in a fairytale (or special temporary circumstances), can that happen. This doesn't mean the villains of my narrative are bad people; many are quite decent and intelligent, like you, Murray. It means that the mission of ambition and survival trumps a commitment to excellence every time.

It's an ancient problem. Gym teachers and math teachers become principals and administrators because they have the least work to do in a school day, the least stress, and they pay the least emotional toll in doing it. They have time to feather their nests. Climbing the pyramid, they surround themselves with loyal friends as buffers, always careful to include representatives of any special interest that might upset the cozy arrangements.

School as Narcotic

What have we done, Murray? Filling blackboards and workbooks, running videos, cramming heads with disconnected information we have driven even the idea of quality from the field. And by constantly bathing the young in passivity, showering them with petty orders and bells for their own good, we have created a foundry where incomplete men and women are forged.

Our school products emerge with only shaky grasp of the past, with a void where comprehension should be; they have no capacity to visualize the future. Every single secondary school student in New York City is taught that North and South Vietnam are one country, divided, and all their teachers believe that, too. But the truth is that for *thousands* of years they were *three* countries — and only forced together for a short time under French domination. The civilization of the two northern countries, Annam and Tonkin, derives largely from China; the culture of South Vietnam, a country know as Champa, comes — like that of Cambodia — from India. The two regions have been fighting for nearly two thousand years. Like the Sunnis and the Shiites in the artificial country fabricated by the British called Iraq, there is no "solution" to the conflict — only violence periodically renewed. Why don't you know this, Murray? Your license says you are a "history teacher," but what you teach is official propaganda.

Nightmare children are all about us, diseased by our indifference; some have capacity to heal themselves, most don't. These are nightmare children, I say; no vital interests, creatures trained to organize their time around spasms of excitement and amusement, or escape from punishment. The maps of the road ahead we gave them in school are false. The most curious commentary on these kids is the thousands of hours they spend in *not* exploring, *not* playing, not seeking opportunities for personal gain — *but in watching other people on television, in music videos and computer games.*

Sane children would never do this — the arc of anyone's life is too short to accept passivity and fantasy to this degree. Conjure with these numbers: in families where the husband and wife have never been divorced, and where the wife doesn't work, the index of spectatorship — TV and otherwise — drops to one-tenth the big-city average.

The institution you and I work for creates addiction. It addicts children to prefer thin abstraction and dull fantasies to reality. As I've grown older I've come to believe that good teachers are more dangerous than bad ones. They keep this sick institution alive.

Old friend, I'm done. I'm going to circulate this letter to the new school board in the hopes it might make some of them think. I haven't the slightest reason to believe it will, but that doesn't excuse me from trying.

5

Hector Isn't the Problem

I Quit

During my thirtieth year as a schoolteacher in Community School District Three, Manhattan, after teaching in all five secondary schools in the district and crossing swords with one professional administration after another as they strove to rid themselves of me; after having my license suspended twice for insubordination and covertly terminated once while I was on medical leave of absence; after the City University of New York borrowed me for a five-year stint as lecturer in its education department; (where I ranked first among 250 education faculty in the "Student-Faculty Ratings" each year I was there); after planning and bringing about the most successful permanent school fundraiser in New York City history; after helping a single eighth-grade class perform thirty thousand hours of volunteer community service; after organizing and financing a student-run food cooperative, securing more than a thousand apprenticeships, and directing the collection of tens of thousands of books for the construction of private student libraries; after producing four talking job dictionaries for the blind, writing two original student musicals and launching an armada of other initiatives to reintegrate students into a larger human reality — I quit.

I was New York State Teacher of the Year when it happened. An accumulation of disgust and frustration that grew too heavy is what finally did me in. To test my resolve, I sent a short essay to the *Wall Street Journal* titled, "I Quit, I Think." In it, I explained my reasons for deciding to throw in the towel, despite having no savings and not the slightest idea what else I might do in my mid-fifties to pay the rent. The essay, in its entirety, read:

> Government schooling is the most radical adventure in history. It kills the family by monopolizing the best times of childhood and by teaching disrespect for home and parents. The whole blueprint of school procedure is Egyptian, not Greek or Roman. It grows from the theological idea that human value is a scarce thing, represented symbolically by the narrow peak of a pyramid.
>
> That idea passed into American history through the Puritans. It found it's "scientific" presentation in the bell curve, along which talent supposedly apportions itself by some iron law of biology. It's a religious notion, and school is its church. I offer rituals to keep heresy at bay. I provide documentation to justify the heavenly pyramid.
>
> Socrates foresaw that if teaching became a formal profession, something like this would happen. Professional interest is served by making what is easy to do seem hard; by subordinating the laity to the priesthood. School is too vital a jobs project, contract giver, and protector of the social order to allow itself to be "re-formed." It has political allies to guard its marches; that's why reforms come and go without altering much. Even reformers can't imagine school being much different.
>
> David learns to read at age four; Rachel, at age nine: In normal development, when both are thirteen, you can't tell which one learned first — the five-year spread means nothing at all. But in school, I label Rachel "learning disabled" and slow David down a bit, too. For a paycheck, I teach David to depend on me to tell him when to go and stop. He won't outgrow that dependency. I identify Rachel as discount mer-

chandise, "special education" fodder. She'll be locked in her place forever.

In thirty years of teaching kids, rich and poor, I almost never met a learning-disabled child; hardly ever met a gifted-and-talented one, either. Like all school categories, these are sacred myths created by human imagination. They derive from questionable values that we never examine because they preserve the temple of schooling.

That's the secret behind short-answer tests, bells, uniform time blocks, age grading, standardization, and all the rest of the school religion punishing our nation. There isn't a right way to become educated; there are as many ways as there are fingerprints. We don't need state-certified teachers to make education happen — certification probably guarantees it won't.

How much more evidence is necessary? Good schools don't need more money or a longer year; they need real free-market choices, variety that speaks to every need and runs risks. We don't need a national curriculum or national testing either. Both initiatives arise from ignorance of how people learn or deliberate indifference to it. I can't teach this way any longer. If you hear of a job where I don't have to hurt kids to make a living, let me know. Come fall, I'll be looking for work.

My little essay went off in March, and I forgot it. Somewhere along the way, I must have gotten a note saying it would be published at the editor's discretion, but if so, it was quickly forgotten in the press of turbulent feelings that accompanied my own internal struggle. Finally, on July 5, 1991, I swallowed hard and quit. Twenty days later, the *Journal* published the piece.

~

Looking back on a thirty-year teaching career full of rewards and prizes, somehow I can't completely believe that I spent so much of my time on earth institutionalized. I can't believe that centralized schooling is allowed to exist at all as a gigantic indoctrination and sorting machine, robbing people of their children. Did it really happen? Was this my life? God help me.

School is a religion. Spinoza knew that. Without understanding this holy-mission aspect, you'll be certain to mistake its contradictions as products of stupidity, venality, or classs warfare. All are present, but none counts for much. School would move in the same direction regardless.

Ordinary people send their children to school to get smart, but what modern schooling teaches is dumbness. Old-fashioned dumbness used to be simple ignorance. Now it's been transformed into permanent mathematical categories of relative stupidity, such as "gifted and talented," "mainstream," and "special ed" — categories in which learning is rationed for the good of the system and the social order. Dumb people are no longer merely ignorant. Now they are dangerous imbeciles whose minds must be conditioned with substantial doses of commercially prepared disinformation for tranquilizing purposes.

The new dumbness is particularly deadly to middle- and upper-middle-class kids already made shallow by the pressures to conform imposed by the world on their often lightly rooted parents. When these kids come of age, they feel certain they must know something, because their degrees and licenses say they do. They remain convinced of this until an unexpectedly brutal divorce, a corporate downsizing, or panic attacks brought on by meaninglessness manage to upset the precarious balance of their incomplete adult lives. Alan Bullock, the English historian, said evil is a state of incompetence. If he's right, then our school adventure filled the twentieth century with evil.

Once the best children are broken to such a system, they disintegrate morally, becoming dependent on group approval. A National Merit Scholar in my own family once wrote that her dream was to be "a small part in a great machine." It broke my heart. What kids dumbed down by schooling can't do is think for themselves or ever be at rest very long without feeling crazy; stupefied boys and girls reveal their dependence in many ways and are easily exploited by their knowledgeable elders.

If you believe nothing can be done for the dumb except kindness, because it's biology (the bell-curve model); if you believe capitalist oppressors have ruined the dumb (the neo-Marxist model); if you believe the dumbness reflects depraved moral fiber (the Calvinist model), or is nature's way of disqualifying boobies from the reproduction sweepstakes (the Darwinian model), or society's way of providing someone to clean your toilet (the pragmatic-elitist model), or that it's evidence of bad karma (the Buddhist model); if you believe any of the various explanations given for the position of the dumb in the social order, then you will be forced to concur that a vast bureaucracy is necessary to address the problem of the dumb. Otherwise they would murder us in our beds.

The possibility that dumb people don't exist in sufficient numbers to warrant the many careers devoted to tending them may seem incredible to you. Yet that is my proposition: mass dumbness first had to be imagined; it isn't real.

Hector, the Horse-Tamer

See thirteen-year-old Hector Rodriguez as I first saw him one cold November day: slightly built, olive-skinned, short, with huge black eyes, his body twisted acrobatically in an attempt to slip past the gate of the skating rink at the northern end of Central Park. I had known Hector for several months as his teacher, but up to that time I had never really *seen* him, nor would I have seen him then but for the startling puzzle he presented: he was gate-crashing with a fully paid admission ticket in his pocket. Was he nuts?

Finding Hector wedged between the bars of the revolving security gate, I yelled, "Hector, you idiot, why are you sneaking in? You have a ticket!"

He gave me a look that said, "Why shout? I know what I'm doing." He actually appeared offended by my lack of understanding.

Hector was conducting an experiment to answer a simple question: Could the interlocking bars of the automatic turnstile be defeated? What safer way to find out than with a paid ticket in hand in case he got caught?

Later, as I searched school records for clues to understanding this boy, I discovered that, in his short time on earth, he had built up a long record as an outlaw. Although none of his crimes would have earned him more than a good spanking a hundred years earlier, now they helped support a social-service empire.

At the time of this incident, Hector attended one of the lowest-rated public schools in New York State, part of a select group threatened with takeover by state overseers. Of the thirteen classes in Hector's grade, a full nine were of higher rank than the one he was in. Hector was an exhausted salmon swimming upstream in a raging current that threatened to sweep away his dignity. We had deliberately unleashed the flood by assigning about eleven hundred kids to five strict categories: "gifted and talented honors;" "gifted and talented;" "special progress;" "mainstream;" and "special ed." (These last kids had a cash value to the school three times higher than that of the others, providing a genuine incentive to find fatal defects where none existed.)

Hector belonged to the doomed category called "mainstream," itself further divided into subcategories labeled A, B, C and D. Worst of the worst, above special ed, was mainstream D. This was where Hector reported. Since special ed was a life sentence of ostracism and humiliation at the hands of one's peers, we might even call Hector lucky to be in mainstream, though as mainstream D, he was suspended in that thin layer of mercy just above the truly doomed. Hector's standardized-test scores placed him about three years behind the middle of the pack. He wasn't just behind the eight ball; he was six feet under it.

Shortly after I found Hector breaking and entering, he was arrested in a nearby elementary school with a gun. It was a fake gun, but it looked pretty real to the school's secretaries and principal. Hector had been dismissed for the Christmas holiday that morning, at which time he had high-tailed it to his old elementary school (which was still in session), intending to turn the younger children loose, to free the slaves like a pint-sized Spartacus. I found this out at the faculty Christmas party when the principal came over to where I was camped by the potato salad and cried, "Gatto, what have you done to me?"

Travel forward now one year in time: Hector is a freshman in high school. On his second report card, he has failed every subject and has been absent enough to be cited for truancy.

Can you see the Hector portrayed by these implacable school records? Poor, small for his age, a member of a minority, not paid much attention by people who matter, dumb in a superdumb class, a bizarre gate-crasher, a gunslinger, a total failure in high school. Can you see Hector? Certainly you think you can. How could you not? The system makes it so easy to classify him and predict his future.

What is society to do with its Hectors? This is the boy, multiplied by millions, whom school people agonized about in every decade of the twentieth century. This is the boy who destroyed the academic mission of American public schooling, turning it into a warehouse operation, a clinic for behavioral training and attitude adjustment. When the *Christian Science Monitor* made a documentary about my class and Hector's, the principal said to the filmmakers, "Sure, the system stinks, but John has nothing to replace it. And as bad as the system is, it's better than chaos."

But is the only alternative to a stifling system really chaos? The country has been sold the idea Hector is the problem of modern schooling. That misperception is the demon we face, under its many guises and behind its shape-shifting rhetoric. Forced schooling itself was conceived to be the front line in a war against chaos, the beginning of the effort to keep Hector and his kind in protective custody. Important people believe, with the fervor of religious zealots, that civilization can survive only if the irrational, unpredictable impulses of human nature are continually beaten back and confined until their demonic vitality is sapped.

6

The Camino de Santiago

Feedback

Let me confess from the start I'm on the board of advisors of an organization called TV-Free America. As a schoolteacher I found that the kids who drove me crazy were always big TV watchers. Their behavioral profile wasn't pretty. TV-addicted kids were irresponsible, childish, dishonest, malicious to one another; above all else they seemed to lack any sustaining purpose of their own, as if by consuming too many made-up stories, modeling themselves after too many men and women who were pretending to be somebody else, listening to too many talking hamburgers and too many explanations of the way things are (sponsored by oil companies and dairy councils) they had lost the power to behave with integrity — to grow up.

It was almost as if by stealing time children needed to write their own stories, television — like school itself — had dwarfed their spirits. When computers came along, I saw they often made the problem worse. Potentially, they were a better deal, because of the capacity to offer interactivity, but a majority of users I saw wallowed in porno, games spent playing against programs, not other people, and many spectator pursuits which required only consumption, not actively-committed behavior.

Even with the Internet I saw how easy it was to cross the line into a passive state unless good discipline was exercised, and I knew from experience how hard that was to come by.

Casting about for a working hypothesis with which to fashion antidotes to the damage, I quickly abandoned preaching as a solution. Whatever could be said against TV, games, the Internet, and all the rest, had been said to these kids so many times their minds refused to hear the words anymore. Relief would have to come from a different quarter; if these things were truly bad as I believed, if they diminished the intellect and corrupted the character as I felt, a solution would have to be found *in the natural proclivity of the young to move around physically*, not sit, before we suppress that urge with confinement to seats in school and with commercial blandishments to watch performers rather than to perform oneself.

The master mechanism at work to cause harm was a suppression of natural feedback circuits which allow us to learn from our mistakes. Somebody trying to learn to sail alone in a small boat will inevitably tack too far left and too far right when sailing into a wind, when the destination is straight ahead, but practice will correct that beginner's error because feedback will instruct the sailor's reaction and judgement. In the area of mastering speech, with all its complex rhythms of syntax, and myriad notes and tones of diction, the most crucial variable is time spent in practice. And in both instances the more challenging the situation, the quicker that competence is reached.

The principal reason bureaucracies are so stupid is that they cannot respond efficiently to feedback. Think of school management, compelled by law to follow *rules* made long ago and far away — as if human situations are so formulaic they can be codified. Management resents feedback from parents, teachers, students, or outside criticism because its internal cohesion depends upon rules, not give and take.

The absolute necessity for feedback from everywhere in taking an education, (even from one's enemies), forced me to look closely at how rigidly students were ordered about — in a way which made little use of their innate abilities to grow through feedback. My guess was that by restoring this natural biological circuitry, the hideous displays of media-sickened behavior among my students would decline. And the guess proved right.

Now you have the information you need to understand what made my Guerrilla Curriculum different from garden-variety "alternative" approaches — its target was inactivity (and even activity which didn't significantly call feedback into play). Sufficient activity, all by itself and aimed in *any* direction, would cause the kids to voluntarily cut back on time spend staring at lighted boxes. My strong hunch was that the childish expressions of children had little to do with the content of media programming, and everything to do with a fatal calculus in which real experience is subtracted from young lives, and simulated experience added in its place.

I set out to shock my students into discovering that face-to-face engagement with reality was more interesting and rewarding than watching the pre-packaged world of media screens, my target was helping them jettison the lives of spectators which had been assigned to them, so they could become players. I couldn't tell anyone in the school universe what I was doing, but I made strenuous efforts to enlist parents as active participants. Just as Shen Wenrong broke many laws to bring the Phoenix steel plant to Shanghai three times faster than German engineers thought it could be done, I broke many to put this Guerrilla Curriculum into effect. From the first it delivered heartening results.

Plunging kids into the nerve-wracking, but exhilarating waters of real life — sending them on expeditions across the state, opening the court systems to their lawsuits, and the economy to their businesses, filling public forums with their speeches and political action — made them realize, without lectures, how much of their time was customarily wasted sitting in the dark. And as that realization took hold, their dependence on the electronic doll houses diminished.

The Camino de Santiago

An important inspiration for this transformational curriculum came from a medieval pilgrimage road across northern Spain called the Camino de Santiago. Every year thousands of well educated, often accomplished people from all over the world, walk hundreds of miles along the way to the burial place of the Apostle James in Santiago de Compostela, a city in northwestern Spain. The custom began long ago, but in the modern era it has increasingly been adopted by people not religious in the usual sense, modern people estranged by the pressures of contemporary life. They make the pilgrimage to build a new relationship with themselves, to feel self-reliant, to be close to nature, to enjoy history and culture and give them time to reflect on things.

My assumption was that if TV and computers had estranged my kids from themselves, their families, and nature, perhaps a similar pilgrimage could help them find a way to come back. Acting in conspiracy with parents who were as desperate as I was, I sent my 13-year-old students to journey alone on foot through the five boroughs of New York City. Some walked the circumference of Manhattan, a distance of about 30 miles; others walked through different neighborhoods, comparing them, constructing profiles of the people and businesses in each from the clues of dress, speech, architecture, window displays — integrating these first-hand observations with interviews and library research (much of which can be Googled today).

Some kids mapped Central Park in its different aspects, some mapped great university campuses, business districts, churches, museums — some invaded such government departments as the board of education or police headquarters, but not on school trips. Individually. They described and analyzed what they saw there, wrote up guide pamphlets for others, attempted to master the character and utility of these places.

Nobody was forced into doing an expedition alone although that produced the maximum value, but all school year long a standing offer was available that anybody could get a day or two (or ten, although that required more cunning to get past the bureaucracy) away from school to explore something — as long as he or she was willing to walk alone and undertake some useful field of study.

A Visitor's Key to Iceland

Because my son-in-law was an Icelander, I was motivated to learn as much about that remote culture as I could. And in the act of doing private research I came upon another rich source of inspiration for the curriculum I was making up as I went along. Iceland has a weird and wonderful guidebook which someone lent me a copy of, *A Visitor's Key to Iceland*. This unique book follows every road in that country, step by step, bringing the land itself and all its built environment fully alive: two chests of silver are believed hidden in this hill. Here a collapsing bridge allowed a murderer to escape — and proved his innocence! In this hot spring a famous outlaw boiled his meat. Over there is a farm whose occupants refused a pregnant woman shelter — they were buried alive by a landslide that same night.

Here is history at its best, animating everything, bringing the abstract lines on a map or the words in a history book to vivid life. With that model as my example, my kids produced visitor's keys to the safest spots in Manhattan to hide out while playing hooky, to the great pizza parlors of Manhattan (and the rotten ones, too), to the architecture of brownstone apartment buildings in a ten block radius of the school, to the neighborhood swimming pools of the five boroughs (few and far between, but enough for a wonderful comparative guide, complete with sociological analyses of their cultural contexts and clientele). Many experiments involved extracting the hidden knowledge and points of view of old men and women, those confined to homes, and those who spent their time sitting on the benches in Riverside or Central Park.

Once this production-oriented transformation was underway, the glow of radiant screens lost some of its allure; it isn't nearly as rewarding to watch actors as to be in action yourself. Reality, when tied to compelling intellectual work, causes feedback circuits in a majority of the young to produce substantial growth, so much so that I came to expect that the moral and behavioral cripples who walked through my classroom door in September would be well on their way to becoming interesting and productive young people by the following April. I don't want to take credit for what must have been discovered when we lived in caves — accepting hard challenges head on is a *sine qua non* of self-mastery and competence. It isn't rocket science.

The biggest surprise for me was how easy this was to accomplish, it took neither talent nor money; anyone could duplicate my results. I won't deny its *hard* work to try to pull off the trick with 130 kids a year, but a lot of effort is wasted that needn't be in finding ways to circumvent the dead hand of school administration. In a system more congenial to learning (and less to social control) the thrill of doing the labor would more than outweigh the effort required. And, of course, if everyone in the society were on the same page about the necessity of developing intellect and character in the young (not weighting them down with chains), the work would be...child's play.

Over the years my students launched so many useful projects and earned so many plaudits and prizes that I found myself showered with awards from the school establishment which had no idea how I got such results. When I tried to explain to the awards committees how *little* I had to do with the achievements, I suspect it was discounted as obligatory modesty, but these days when I have nothing more to prove to myself about who I am, I sincerely hope you'll believe me. Take your boot off the downtrodden necks of your children, study *their* needs not your own, don't be intimidated by experts, re-connect your kids to primary experience, give off the game of winners and losers for a while, and you'll get the same results I did. Maybe better.

Some inner clock is ticking in every life, warning us we have appointments to keep with reality: real work to do, real skills to learn, real battles to fight, real risks to take, real ideas to wrestle with. And a desperate need to keep death present in your imagination, to never forget how short and inevitable is the arc of your life.

For many years a variety of outside influences — television, computers and government schooling chief among them — have conspired to wean children away from their urgent need to be out and about. The end result has been a nation of angry, frightened, uncompassionate and incomplete boys and girls in place of men and women. People sentenced to be incomplete, incompetent, and fearful will find ways to take vengeance on their neighbors while they continue to die by inches in front of an electronic screen. Restore what has been stolen and the problems of child development warned about by experts will recede, as childhood itself vanishes into the sick Teutonic minds which spawned it.

Since the advent of schoolrooms and electronic screens, many of us never grow up. Too much of our precious trial-and-error period is wasted sitting in the dark. Being a mature being means living with a purpose, your own purpose: it's about welcoming responsibility as the nourishment a big life needs; it's about behaving as a good citizen — finding ways to add value to the community in which you live; it's about wrestling with your weaknesses and developing heart, mind, and spirit — none of them properties of the spectator crowd.

Hitching the body and mind to screens reduces the attention span to quick takes arranged by strangers; it creates a craving for constant stimulation which reality can't satisfy. Violence of one sort or another is the easiest way to still the gnawing hunger for stimulation that the undead feel. And that violence includes the violence of bizarre sex — the most important psychological product vended on the Internet. Russian émigré Pitirim Sorokin, founder of Harvard's sociology department, identified cultures of violence, such as our own, with its insatiable craving for war, as late stages of civilizations in terminal decline.

In all failing societies, respect for obligation and family declines along with compassion for one's fellows — to be replaced by a preoccupation with amusement, diversion, and predation. Despite a carefully calculated propaganda barrage about steadily declining crime rates in recent years, we have four times the rate of violent crime in 1999 than we did in 1959. Four times the number of citizens in jail. These remarkable increases in crime immediately followed the penetration of television into our culture.

As deeply as we seemed mired in these anti-life addictions — being wedded to machinery — ending them is, physically at least, as simple as pulling the plug. Show a TV-addicted young person that life is more interesting than its television substitute and nature will do the rest in time — but the operant term is to "show," not to "tell." Many of my reservations about television apply to computer screens as well. How to avoid becoming an incompletely human extension of this technology while still enjoying its transcendental power to connect us in many new ways, independent of institutional intervention, is the greatest challenge of the 21st century.

If we threw away two of the four high school years and used the money to send everyone walking their own Camino de Santiago, it would help enormously to meet that challenge. It doesn't have to be as spectacular a walk as George Meeghan, the third grade dropout, took when he walked alone from Tierra del Fuego to Point Barrow, Alaska in the 1970s, it needn't be as spectacular a sail as high school dropout Tania Aebi took in the 1980s when she sailed around the world in a 26 foot boat, but there's absolutely no reason every boy and girl in America shouldn't have a significant personal Camino as part of schooling.

If the government won't do that for you, you must do it for yourself.

7

Weapons of Mass Instruction

Only 31 percent of college-educated Americans can fully comprehend a newspaper story, down from 40 percent a decade ago.

— National Commission on the Future of Higher Education, August, 2006

35 percent of the young regret their university experience and don't consider the time and money invested worth it; more than half said they learned nothing of use.

— *Wilson Quarterly*, Autumn 2006

A Moral Odor

At the age of sixteen, a blind French teenager named Jacques Lusseyran became head of an underground resistance group of 600 during WWII. Lusseyran arranged dynamiting, assassinations, and other violent forms of sabotage to free his country from the Germans, a story told in his autobiography, *And Then There Was Light*. In chapter four, he talked about his early schooling, calling the classroom experience a moral disaster:

> ...there is such a thing as moral odor and that was the case at school. A group of human beings that stay in one room

> by compulsion begins to smell. That is literally the case, and with children it happens even faster. Just think how much suppressed anger, humiliated independence, frustrated vagrancy and impotent curiosity can be accumulated by boys between the ages of ten and fourteen…

Lusseyran was able to murder large numbers of men just a few months after he left school "where the world of reality with all its real moral questions was entirely lacking." We become what we behold. It's something to remember, Columbine.

School As A Weapon

Most historical accounts of schooling are so negative you have to wonder how this exercise of pedagogy ever passed the test of time with its original parts nearly unchanged. It must yield some benefits, but what those are and for whom isn't so clear.

It seems obvious that school weakens family and indeed all relationships, but perhaps some valuable trade-off occurs which, on balance, rewards people so radically disconnected from one another and from themselves. School elevates winning so far above its ostensible goal of learning that periodically public scandals occur when investigation reveals that even elite students know very little. A century of lending our children to perfect strangers from an early age — to be instructed in what we aren't quite sure — has made an important statement about modern culture which deserves to be mused upon.

One famous ode of Horace contemplates the torments of schooling. Mosaics at Pompeii illustrate painful episodes of school discipline. Washington Irving's story of the headless horseman celebrates turning the tables big-time on an insufferable schoolmaster. The immortal WWI-era song, "Schooldays, Schooldays, Dear Old Golden Rule Days," describes with affection a relationship between school learning and the "tune of the hickory stick." A recent Hollywood film, *Teaching Miss Tingle*, is about a schoolteacher kidnapped by her students who torture her physically and psychologically. Numerous websites exist which specialize in ways to disrupt school routines. On the other side, we rarely hear anyone attributing their success to school time.

The notion of school as a dangerous place is well-established then, even if the troubling metaphor of weaponry deliberately brought to bear to cause student harm isn't yet widespread. That school can and does inflict damage is no longer surprising although precisely how that happens is only impressionistically understood. And "why" not at all.

This chapter will seek to nail down some specific aspects of the punitive machinery. It won't be comprehensive — you will have weapons of your own to add — nor will I try to rank the ones I give you in any formal order of importance, much of that will depend upon the nature of your own kids, but I feel compelled to plant this flag firmly while I have time left — school is not a good place for your kids. If they are swarmed by friends and win every award the place can offer it changes nothing. From the first month of my teaching career of 30 years, I realized that intellectual power, creative insight, and good character were being diminished in my classroom and that indeed I had been hired for precisely that purpose. I was a clerk in a vast penitentiary; the rules and procedures were the guards.

A Personal Formula

In a short time I became determined to sabotage the system as Lusseyran had sabotaged the Nazi system, peacefully in most instances, but as time passed and my contempt deepened, by small acts of violence as well. In the course of continuous trial-and-error experimentation (behind the façade of being an "English" teacher), I stumbled upon a formula to change the destiny of students, one at a time, the way beached starfish have to be rescued. It required assembling a fairly accurate biography of every individual student from birth onward, all the key people, relationships, experiences, places, opinions, accomplishments and failures. School records and memories weren't good enough, though sometimes there was no alternative. The best data came from parents, grandparents, brothers, sisters, friends and enemies — anyone who could provide intimate information to the emerging personal narrative.

With a rich profile in hand a personal course could be custom-tailored for each kid, put together in partnership with the student, flexible enough to allow constant feedback to change the design, something schools could not do (nor would they if they could). When you believe in determinism — biological, psychological, sociological, or theological (and schools believe in all of those in various times and places), the very idea of feedback leading to growth must be held at arm's length. For all its legends of social mobility and intellectual growth, school operates out of a belief in social order — that all is for the best in this best of all possible worlds.

Once a profile was created, the second step was to add a personalized Wishes and Weaknesses component. I asked each student to list three things each wanted to be knowledgeable about by the end of the year — that was the wishes part — and three weaknesses he or she wished to overcome, deficiencies which led to humiliation (I get beat up all the time) or failures of opportunity (I want to do modeling work but only the rich kids know how to present themselves to get that) — that was the weaknesses part. I exercised virtually no censorship and whatever the individual kid's priorities were became mine. I didn't consult with a single school administrator to put this program in place, nor with any other teacher — only with parents from whom I extracted promises of silence.

I know this sounds like a hideous amount of effort, and politically impossible in a large urban school, but it was neither: it required only will, imagination, resourcefulness, and a determination to scrap any rules which stood in the way — just as Shen Wenrong had done in moving Phoenix. Acting in my favor was the fact that with this new curriculum each kid was motivated, worked much harder than I legally could have asked him or her to do, and recruited outside assistance with resources no classroom teacher could match. And now for the first time each had a personal reason to work hard, one that was self-grading.

As for myself, I became determined to figure out where this bizarre institution had actually come from, why it had taken the shape it did all around the world in the same century, why it was able to turn away intense criticism and grow larger, more expensive, and more intrusive into personal lives. If you allow imagination to work on the institution, it is much more a piece of utopian science fiction, oblivious to human needs, than it is a response to popular demand. Right from the early days of my teaching life, I began a project of research which involved reading and arguing with thousands of books, many dreadfully written and some quite obscure, travelling (by now) three million miles around the country and the world to observe, argue, and discuss schools and which resulted a few years ago in a monster book, still in print, called *The Underground History of American Education*. A major publisher paid me an enormous amount of money to write it (enormous for a schoolteacher) and then refused to publish it after holding it off the market for over a year. "It would embarrass friends of the house," I was told. If you wonder what that might mean, consider this was one of the top three textbook publishing houses too, apart from their trade division.

In this way my schoolteaching practices were directed by intense research on the one hand, and equally intensive and daring field exercises around the city of New York — at times up to sixty different studies in sixty different locations! Simultaneously! Either singly, in small teams, or en masse, "Gatto's Guerrillas," as we called ourselves, infiltrated without notice (or permission either), into public meetings, exhibitions, scheduled hearings, auctions, courthouses, workplaces — anywhere opportunity presented itself. We took public opinion polls on every subject under the sun — often competing with professional news organizations. Travelling dramatic troupes (always more than one) gave shows in elementary schools, in acting studios, and everyplace verbal engagement was possible.

The general targets were many: independence, self-reliance, strategic planning, a good command of the active literacies of speaking and writing, courage, curiosity, an ability to write a script for one's own life.

A major goal was examining barriers schooling creates which restrict intellectual and behavioral superiority to a relative handful of its clientele. Producing a clear inventory of school practices which act to interdict normal development — like involuntary confinement, involuntary associations, bells, bathrooms passes, continuous competitions complete with petty prizes, testing, and all the rest, and discussing the genesis of each, proved useful in changing the way kids approached the school experience. They grew willing to assume full responsibility for educating themselves, in spite of school — rather than trusting an army of strangers to do the job for them. It was a revolution in outlook.

Bad Intentions

I had been hired as an English teacher, but since absolutely nothing was rationally proscribed under a mandate to increase facility with the English language, and since nobody paid close attention to what was happening, if my classes weren't unduly disruptive and parents didn't complain, I put an examination of the public assumptions of schooling at the heart of what I taught. Without ever actually asserting that school was a place of bad intentions I set out to demonstrate to students and their families that the poor results of schooling — with language proficiency, for instance — weren't inevitable, but the results of procedures enshrined in regulation and law.

The system was principally at fault, a conclusion many had reached before me, but not so commonly available was the insight that systems incorporate ways to defend internal integrity. No system will allow deviant behavior. All elements obey central directives or the logic of systematicization vanishes. Course correction by unmediated feedback is powerfully discouraged in any system, even made illegal. By destroying possibilities of internal dialectic, and by concealing the operations of management from public scrutiny, schools render themselves virtually immune to change.

It's not my intention to conjure up dark conspiracies; men and women who staff institutional schooling are very like those in other complex institutions — if they exercise significant free will they become outlaws who must be sanctioned and things which improve performance are hardly more welcome than things which impair it. Deviations from a steady state jeopardize the system mission. Medieval craft guilds in precious metals, stained glass, candle-making, etc. were very much like this: innovation was powerfully resisted, independent practitioners were sanctioned — ostracized if they persisted.

Robert Michel, the French social thinker, investigated bureaucracies more than a century ago and concluded that, without exception, their nominal missions — defending the country, delivering the mail, collecting garbage, etc.—were always secondary to the primary mission: preserving the bureaucracy.

In this regard school is only one of many institutions in American society patterned after a scheme to confuse the public, one first put in place in ancient Sparta — management by cleverly contrived illusions.

Our economy has become rooted in financial trickery. It moves from bubble to bubble in ways which gladden the hearts of speculators privy to the formula — boom and bust the public calls it. When creating bubbles is temporarily ill-advised, wars are invented to fill the temporary bubble-vacuum, although wholesale destruction of property and life occasioned by warfare may be seen as a bubble itself — like our world-famous dream industries; motion picture, television and pop music, just another entertainment to fill up the emptiness of modern life and give it savor. In a nation whose economy depends on bubble illusions, why should the school institution assigned to train the young be any different?

Deliberate Deprivations

In his immortal book, *Wealth of Nations*, Adam Smith — the Scottish philosopher we regard as the father of capital "C" capitalism — made the distinction between education and schooling very clear. At no time did Smith claim education had anything at all to do with national prosperity, only free trade (competition unfettered by excessive rules) and a division of labor contributed to that.

The role of education, said Smith, was needed to compensate for mutilations inflicted as by-products of those same processes which produce wealth. We need to understand that artificial environments produced by free trade and constant competition cause psychological damage in four ways: (1) they make workers cowardly, (2) stupid, (3) sluggish, (4) and indifferent to everything but animal needs. Only education (he called it "educational schooling") will heal the wounds to community and individuality caused by capitalism.

According to the father of capitalism, the only differences between children of philosophers and those of street sweepers lies in the training they receive. All children, he asserts, have the talents we associate with elite families, all, that is, until the majority of young are deliberately deprived of "subject(s) for thought and speculation." Those so deprived become "deformed," unable to bear hard thinking. They lose "power of judgment, even as regards ordinary matters." He could have been describing public school kids in 2009.

The new curriculum I devised toward the end of the 1960s was intended as a counterattack on cowardice, stupidity, sluggishness, and indifference. It had nothing to do with test scores. The best work I did as a teacher always consisted of the same priorities: entering a personal partnership with anybody who showed a determination to become educated, then working inside that partnership to help meet specific targets the student set. Those too broken to want an education, I schooled. Over time a fraction of those were inspired by the example of more-enterprising classmates and wanted out of the school routines, too; others were unable to recover. Those I consoled by schooling them as elite children are schooled, by drill long and strong.

Adam Smith was right. Between children identified as bright by schools and those identified as stupid, hardly a difference exists but those created by deliberate deprivation.

The House of Mirrors

In one of the strange ironies of history, Adam Smith's own publisher, William Playfair, chided Smith for his innocence. The social order to which he and Smith belonged was held together by deliberately depriving most people of information they needed to maximize opportunities. If secrets were promiscuously distributed, the ladders of privilege would collapse, their own children would be plunged back into the common stew. It was unthinkable. The familiar expression, "a little knowledge is a dangerous thing" was Playfair's invention. "Proper" schooling teaches "negatively," it never allows the working classes or the poor "to read sufficiently well to understand what they do read."

Set down clearly over 200 years ago, here is the recipe for the schools we commonly experience. Playfair argued that public instruction would ruin national prosperity, not enhance it. And who is to say he is wrong as long as prosperity is reckoned in dollars and cents. "The education of the middling and lower ranks" has to be put aside, to be replaced with psychological conditioning in habits and attitudes of deference, envy, appetite, and mistrust of self, if the system of capitalism is to survive with all the benefits it provides.

"A smattering of learning is a very dangerous thing," he said, not because ordinary people are too dumb to learn; just the opposite, they are too smart to be allowed to learn. People become dangerous when too many see through the illusions which hold society together.

Long ago in China, Playfair's philosophy had been given a name by the emperors in pre-history. It was called "The Policy of Keeping People Dumb." The only change the passage of millennia brought in this leadership perspective was in the form of a change in style — in the modern era leaders no longer spoke openly about this great secret of management.

The Lincoln Elective Program

Lincoln Academy, New York City, 1985. A public junior high school, despite its fancy name, located next door to a housing project for the poor, far from the center of Manhattan's dynamic Upper West Side. The West Side of Manhattan is world-famous, a zone of substantial accomplishment, wealth, and power. Home to Columbia University; Fordham; Julliard; Barnard; the Jewish Theological Seminary;

Columbia Teachers College; Riverside Church; The Lincoln Center: The Metropolitan Opera; The Symphony; The Museum of Natural History; and the Historical Society. Bounded on the east by Central Park, on the west by Riverside Park — one of the great intellectual centers of the earth, housing twenty-odd public schools.

If government schooling were intended to succeed anywhere, it would have to be here, inside this micro-environment of wealth, talent, taste, enlightenment, and European liberal tradition. Yet inside Intermediate School 44 on West 77th Street where I taught for 16 years, bands of marauders roamed the corridors (like my own shown in the photograph on the back cover); three rapes took place inside a single week; and bandit gangs from a nearby high school beat and robbed other students at will.

No dangerous event was ever reported to police, no general caution to parents that safety could not be guaranteed was ever issued, the moral odor of institutional bureaucracy reeked like a dead fish in School District Three, a place many believed the moral center of progressivism in the United States. District Three was a bedroom community for television, theatre and the arts, yet giant firecrackers went off randomly inside the quietly surreal school building on West 77th Street, while opposite the school, not a hundred feet from it, rents climbed beyond a thousand dollars a room per month and kept climbing to double (and nearly triple) that for a one-room studio.

By the 1980s, when I transferred to Lincoln Academy, central management in District Three was employing aggressive reform rhetoric. New programs were regularly announced: partnerships with Columbia, Fordham, the Ford Foundation, the mayor's office, and various federal agencies, and an elective program, intended we were told to bring students into the management loop by giving them a part in decision-making was launched. Like 700 other teachers in the district I was ordered to prepare curriculum for an elective of my own design. It was to be a study of epic poetry from Homer through Milton to Tennyson.

On the first day I met my elective, faces were visibly unhappy; on the second revolt reared its head — my offering clearly wasn't congenial to anyone except myself. Why had they chosen to be there? I asked for written explanations:

Tonya—I had no choice. They chose it for me.

Gloria — They said to come in here. I didn't even know what it meant. That's why I'm here.

Eddie — I wanted soccer. The only reason I have this is because Dean picked it for me.

Francisco — I am here because Dean said I had to be.

Jane — Dean said this was the only elective I could pick.

Tanisha— I picked this because Dean picked it for me.

Tamura — I am here because Dean ordered me.

Jose — Dean put me here.

George — I didn't pick it. Dean picked it for me.

Bonnie — The principal picked it.

Sunt lacrimae rerum et mentum mortalia tangent

Contempt

In March of 2005, Indiana University released a study of school-based anti-smoking programs — which cost taxpayers huge sums of money every year. California alone has invested over a half-billion dollars on this effort. Is the money well-spent?

According to the abstract of the report printed in the *International Herald Tribune* for March 24, 2005, the principal author, Dr. Sarah Wiehe, said that all such programs have one common characteristic — they all fail. "It may be," said Dr. Wiehe, "that any program conducted in schools induces contempt in students." You'll want to digest that conclusion slowly, ruminating on its invisible consequences. *As long as school is the delivery vehicle, any undertaking is held in contempt.* But for most of us school exists as the principal forge of intellectual development. Is study itself then brought into contempt?

As that university study was being reported in the European press, Janet and I were in a unique French village near Limoges called Oradour sur Glane, a town without a single inhabitant, all its buildings intact except the ruined church which had been burned to the ground on June 10, 1944, by retreating German military forces in WWII. On that day every single citizen was murdered save one — an eight-year-old boy, Roger Godfrin, who disobeyed his schoolteachers when they obeyed German orders to bring their classes to the town square and church. "Hurry! Hurry!" Roger remembers them saying, "Don't keep them waiting!" Without his contempt for school, which led him to run away and hide instead, Roger would have burned to ashes with the rest.

Irrelevance

Why has schooling acquired such a bad odor? Part of the answer lies in the political nature of mass schooling — a characteristic inherent in any bureaucracy. It's not so much kids think in these abstract terms, it's the widespread understanding among the young that school isn't about them (and their interests, curiosities and futures), but exclusively about the wishes of other people. School is built around the self-interest of others. What's the point of taking this test or that one? Is there any point at all that any young person with real priorities, real anxieties, and real questions which need to be answered would be likely to accept? How would you personally deal with the assertion, "I don't need to know anything about the Leaning Tower of Pisa!" What would you say? Is it possible the complaint is well founded?

What of the political nature of schooling which allows any group in political control and all its important political rivals to edit out any teaching which might call its own privileges, practices, or beliefs into question? School has no choice but to limit free thought and speech to such a profound degree a gulf is opened between the sanctimonious homilies of pedagogy ('searching for truth', 'leveling the playing field', etc.) and the ugly reality of its practices. Will you require me to prove that? I hope so. I shall do it with a stark example from Australia in the expectation you will have no trouble transferring the principle learned to America.

The Australian Example

Australia has an ecosystem so delicately balanced that its health or sickness is quickly transferred to every student in every school. Because of that inescapable, ever-present reality, you might imagine government policy toward the environment would provide compelling analytical matter for curriculum in every academic specialty, but if you thought so you would be dead wrong.

One instance will show you why. For years the government there supported a project to eliminate deeply rooted grasses, replacing them with shallowly rooted British grasses which provide food for sheep in a land unsuited to sheep, but where a sheep industry is politically powerful. Sheep chew grass far down; that causes salt to rise from subsoil and concentrate in topsoil — a significant problem for farmers. But something just as bad or worse happens, too: huge quantities of soil blow away and contaminate rivers. Soil-laden water kills fish populations and pollutes the tidal margins where land meets ocean. All over the world this tidal margin is the great producer of fish, but in Australia, with the longest coastline on earth, the tidal zone is the least productive anywhere, in part a result of sheep farming in an environment ill-matched to sheep.

There's more. Tourism, not sheep, is the nation's big money-maker. Among its unique sights is the Great Barrier Reef, a vast mountain of coral harboring a rich collection of sea life. As soil in rivers which flow to the reef has increased, large sections of coral have died, losing their characteristic brilliant red hues which in death change to ugly grey.

Tourism which benefits every corner of the country has been placed in jeopardy to please the sheep lobby. Jared Diamond's *Collapse*, about historical patterns of social collapse, has a long chapter on Australia, including a discussion of the impact of sheep.

But what, you say, does this ongoing tragedy have to do with school affairs? Well, if the degradation of the economy the young must work in isn't considered a suitable subject for study, it's hard to see why the Leaning Tower of Pisa is. The simple truth is that Australian schools will never be allowed to study and debate vital matters, even though they are sentenced to inherit the mess. Now prepare a list of things your own local schools would only take seriously at their own peril. Go ahead, it isn't difficult. Is fast food a major taxpayer in your area? Check and see if *Fast Food Nation* is in the school library, or *Super Size Me* in the film collection. In the history department, what coverage exists of the religious wars between Catholics and Protestants or Christians and Muslims? Does any of it deal with the specifics of doctrinal differences without which essential aspects of human nature are flushed down the toilet even though they bear heavily on America's situation in the world today.

Anyone who reflects on personal experience will acknowledge that ease and sophistication with spoken language is substantially more important in life than reading. What percentage of class time in your school's language classes is set aside for that? Don't bother to answer any of these questions, I know the situation in your school already.

Alfred North Whitehead, one of the best known mathematicians of the twentieth century, contended in his book, *The Aims of Education*, that the most essential form of advanced math apart from arithmetic in modern society is statistical prediction. It's in use on an everyday basis in thousands of practical applications, from political predictions to advising clothing manufacturers what colors will be preferred in the months ahead. The math required to hold this power in one's hands is hardly taxing for people of junior high school age. For ordinary lives, nothing in the world of number beyond arithmetic is remotely as useful; if statistics were the mathematical idea taught, past long division, most students would become more effective for the simple ability to predict with numbers. Check what percentage of your school's math curriculum is devoted to statistics.

Enough said about irrelevance, almost every kid understands that political considerations dictate school time be filled with irrelevance; they just don't understand why, because schools wouldn't dare stress the realities of social class and social engineering.

Social Engineering

Thanks to a 24-year-old college dropout named Mark Zuckerberg who created Facebook, and others like him who founded YouTube, MySpace and other social networks still unmonitored by political authorities or academics, thanks to the World Wide Web and the Internet as platforms for individually generated connections, the power of school as a great dis-connector has been weakened.

These vehicles enable people without any particular status, to hook up with one another; they even allow mixtures of nobodies and somebodies to exchange ideas and plans; they provide a fountain of information which replenishes itself constantly; they encourage creativity among masses consigned by schooling to become reliable consumers. Even though this new force is still in early childhood, already it has caused governments to surrender a great deal of power over their own currencies. It has emboldened accumulations of capital to move at the speed of light from one country to another, destabilizing conventional markets, making national loyalties conditional and patriotism questionable. Thanks to the vast new ball of connections, official truth in every conceivable area is subject to verification by a promiscuous collection of uncertified critics armed with the tools to back up their contrarian critiques.

Thanks to the Internet, the concept of mass schooling by experts is nearly exhausted.

Lying by Omission

Bruno is a college student in Portugal who wrote to me on May 17, 2008 asking for my take on several matters for which his school holds official positions and monitors compliance with its stances through testing. It's a common situation everywhere. These unstated biases presented as gospel truth makes official schooling dangerously anti-educational, yet this phenomenon in action is difficult to detect, and among the young, virtually impossible.

Sometimes these pernicious biases are managed simply by omitting some key piece of information. Such was the case that bothered

Bruno, in a graduate school program purporting to explain the mechanism through which evolution is presumed to work. The letter which follows represents my attempt to introduce Bruno to one of the best-concealed weapons of mass instruction: lying by omission:

> Dear Bruno,
>
> You ask my opinion on Darwin's supposition vs. Wallace's, Darwin contending that biological advance occurs through deadly competitions which over time eliminate the weak from success in reproduction, and Wallace arguing that adaptation and cooperation are the important elements.
>
> I would have no opinion on the relative merits of either, but my guess is that what really interests you is how Darwin became the figure historically remembered and Wallace the one forgotten. On that issue I know a great deal.
>
> The politics of science is a matter which hardly ever takes center stage in academic presentations intended for ordinary students, but since Darwin's ascendency was almost exclusively a matter of who he was and who he knew, while Wallace's decline could have been predicted long before it occurred by knowing his background, let me engage your question through that particular aspect of big science, since it is always present and almost always a matter of the greatest importance. Two excellent critical takes on this which you might want to read are Thomas Kuhn's *The Structure of Scientific Revolutions*, and Robert Scott Root-Bernsteins's *Discovering*.
>
> Back to the Darwin victory. I'm certain you were never told in school that Darwin was supremely wealthy and hung around with the circle around the powerful and influential in many countries. And I'm equally certain you don't know that he was trained as a Church of England priest, not as a scientist. In a short while I'll get to the significance of this data, but for the moment you should reflect on the possible reason your teachers would have in keeping this information from you.

Your school and colleges will also have kept from you that Wallace was from a lowly background; all his best sympathies were with people who worked hard for subsistence wages. Those sympathies might have been dismissed as an eccentricity in a fine scientist except that he carried his convictions into the political arena — enraging the very social classes in which Darwin enjoyed membership.

For example, he was prominent in the land reform movement which asked that ownership be turned over to the tiller. He disdained the British scientific establishment as more a private club for rich dilettantes like Darwin than a workshop for science. Is it far-fetched to think some of this biographical record — in both cases — might have made a difference in their respective receptions?

Push this a bit further. Free trade was a passionate issue in the 19th century among so-called champions of the liberal persuasion. But Wallace wrote passionately against free trade, claiming it inflicted hideous hardships on working people. He advocated female suffrage when that idea was anathema to the elites. He was the Ralph Nader of his day — and yet he was totally dependent on the classes he criticized for a fair hearing among his judges.

All this is vital to a clear consideration of your original question, yet an invisible committee charged with helping you gain education saw fit to move these interesting narratives out of your reach. Some flesh and blood individuals had to make this decision on several levels of your schooling. What I haven't gotten to yet is how seditious Wallace's theory really was to the controlling interests of the British Empire, versus Darwin's which fit squarely on top of the government's plans and justified them.

The sad truth is Wallace was worse than hated by Britain's managerial classes. His talk of "peaceful adaptation" as the way to species improvement ran directly counter to the violent means necessary to create and maintain the British Empire. Darwin's explanation, on the other hand, that continuous competition of a life and death variety was nature's way, put the voice of Science squarely in the camp of imperialism, globalism, racism, colonialism, free trade economics, and much else of moment to the powerful in 19th century Britain. But if life were found to be inherently better where cooperation rules, as Wallace said, the privileged world would turn upside down.

By Darwin's day, among the powerful, Christianity had become merely ceremonial, a dangerous relic of the past to be kept under State control as it was in the Anglican order. But Wallace, although not arguing his case from any theological perspective, still marshaled his theory in a way which led to the age-old Christian conclusion: we are our brother's keeper; patience, not violent action, is the wisest course in the face of the inevitable.

The revolutionary ability of the Christian message to stir up the masses and put them maddeningly out of reach of carrot/stick control machinery was regarded with horror by the British upper classes. When people build the meaning of their days out of relationships, love, piety, loyalty, and frugal self-sufficiency, the notion of happiness through an accumulation of stuff suffers. But what were the ramifications of that for a commercial civilization? On the other hand, when competition is seen as essential to a good life, when winning against one's neighbors is put at the heart of society, business thrives. To win, others have to lose: the more losers, the better winning feels.

My dear Bruno, you could build a bridge to the moon and back on the corpses which accrued from Darwin's contentious work and the work of his first cousin, Francis Galton, in initiating out the politics of his biological suppositions. He provided policymakers already disposed to regard the mass population as "human resources," with justification for disregarding the silly idea of human rights. Most people were evolutionary dead-ends, Darwin had spoken, just as had Fichte, Spinoza, Calvin, and Plato before him when they said much the same thing. Or the Anglican theory of a Divine Order, for that matter. Apologists today will protest that the damage has been caused by "Social Darwinists" who hammered his ideas into practical directives for the management of society, but don't let them fool you. You need only read *Descent of Man* to see that Darwin himself was the master Social Darwinist, even if it was his cousin who invented the new science of "eugenics" to provide the same options with human beings for social leaders as they already had in plant and animal breeding.

I hope this sheds some light on Wallace's eclipse. His public attacks on military spending alone would have been enough to doom him to obscurity. I'm surprised he gets the footnote in scientific history he does, but I expect that will vanish, too, at some not too distant moment in the future. Take this single example as a specimen of the illusions which control the public imagination.

Building Bombs

Ninety-eight years ago as I write, anybody who had access to the *Encyclopedia Britannica* (11th edition) could have learned how to produce powerful explosives cheaply and with ordinary materials — from combustible dust explosives whose power is derived from finely ground corn in gaseous form, or table sugar, to even more powerful fertilizer bombs, based on ammonium nitrate and diesel oil. The truck bomb which destroyed the government building in Oklahoma City is in the encyclopedia, and others as well.

But no small farmer would have needed to read it there because for everyone who wanted to know about such things, the information was widely available.

Even today, such information isn't hard to come by if you want it. The formula for the TATP bomb which closed the London Underground in 2005 was soon afterwards publicly available (unwittingly, I suppose) in the influential *Financial Times* — on its editorial page! The only significant information missing from the *FT* account was supplied a little while later on the *New York Times* editorial page, in the form of a display advertisement from an Israeli company selling bomb-detection machines. You could hardly deprive the public of bomb-making materials, even if you wanted to:

The Recipe:

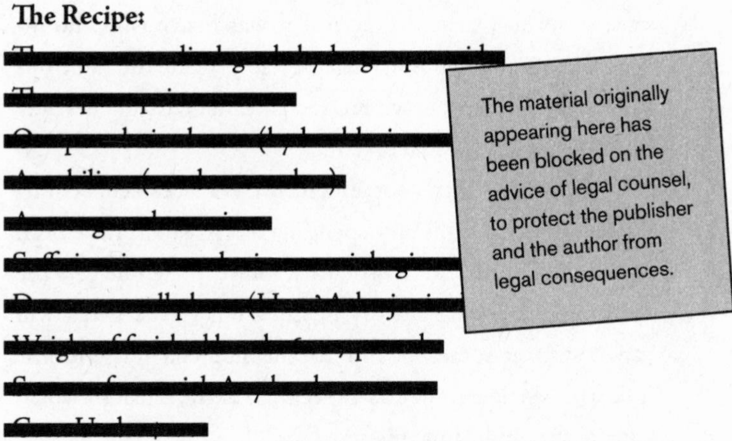

Why would anyone with decent motives *want* such information? Only a population broken to its own insignificance would ask such a slavish question. For anyone who understands what the miracle of America once was (and is no more), that it was a forge to convert slaves, serfs, peasants, and proletarians into free men and women, explosives were an important part of self-reliance and liberty. They were important tools in clearing land, digging foundations, constructing ponds, building roads, moving stones, digging gold mines — perhaps in the gravest extreme even defending your family's liberty from agents of the political state. Isn't that how we got a United States in the first place? Because the common population was armed? Has the possibility of a tyranny here miraculously vanished? But violent conflict aside, and melodrama with it, the tool aspect alone ought to be the common right of free citizens. And whether you agree or not isn't as important as realizing that less than a hundred years ago, perfectly ordinary people were trusted to handle power like this with responsibility.

What has changed in the intervening century? Have ordinary people become more dangerous, or have governments demanded exclusive ownership of things which might unseat them? Carroll Quigley, professor of international relations at Georgetown and former personal tutor of president Clinton's when Clinton attended that school, wrote in *Tragedy and Hope: A History of the World in Our Time* that the rights of ordinary people thrive at those times when common citizens are well armed against the incursions of their own government — and that liberty declines precipitously when arms are denied the commonality. Adolf Hitler's first act in office was to ban possession of firearms among citizens.

Once again you'll want to know what information like this has to do with schooling and at the risk of insulting you I'll reply that only a man or woman whose imagination has been ruined, only someone who traded self-respect for security long ago, would need an explanation. These are among the hundreds, perhaps thousands of ideas without which education is impossible — you needn't accept one side of the argument or the other to become educated, but you do have to accept that argument about these things is at the core of the matter. You can't win liberty by memorizing what you're told to memorize. "*Nullius in verba*" is the motto of the Royal Scientific Society, founded in 1620, which I translate as "Don't take anybody's word for the truth; think for yourself!" The watchword of school is "Let others think for you."

The Decisive Ratio

The new revolution made possible by factory schooling returned citizenship in libertarian America to a deadly ratio which once existed in classical Greece, Tudor England, and Prussia of the Fredericks — a large number of puppets, a small group of puppet masters. Kids don't understand why it's happening, but they sense themselves being put to death in school. That's why they hate it so much.

Physical Ugliness

You never hear among the common complaints against schooling that it acts as a workshop to create physical and psychological ugliness, but that's exactly what I'm going to say — the habits it inculcates lead to ugliness in a culture where beauty and grace is much more important than school allows you to know.

One great secret which you always suspected I'll confirm for you right now: the physical appearance of human bodies is an important sorting device at elite universities — if you're ugly, ungainly, unathletic, ungraceful, your chances of admission at Yale or Stanford drop almost to zero. Your physical appearance tells a sophisticated observer a great deal about you and whether you might be worthy to carry the institution's flag. Here is one of those hundreds of thousands of ideas which school might spend its time examining, but as with much else, it avoids treating entirely. In this case merely omitting discussion of the ideas involved doesn't do the major damage, much more direct methods are employed to tag you with the stigmata of failure which ugliness signifies.

If you wanted general health and vigor in an oncoming generation, would you enforce immobility on it for twelve to twenty years? Would you tie that immobility to constant stresses created by bells and various threats? Would you add to these handicaps the fat-and sugar-rich diet of school lunches or allow snack wagons and soda pop vendors inside the school orbit? Don't these provide a direct road to overweight and obesity, ill health, weakness, gracelessness, vulgarity and timidity?

It has long been acknowledged that the most powerful prejudice in America is our national hatred of fat people. This, even though more citizens (and students) are fat here than anywhere else on earth. The epidemic nature of this phenomenon robs a significant chunk of graduates of our 12-year training programs in ugliness of dignity, friends, opportunity, romance — it is among the most vicious weapons of mass instruction. Your associates through life will forgive you for being ignorant of quadratic questions — or the Leaning Tower of Pisa, but they will not overlook the sin of your low vitality, or your fatness.

Being fat and ugly lowers your chances for admission to any elite university like Stanford. Evaluation protocols at top colleges prefer good looks, a slender body, and an outgoing personality because they know that those characteristics — together with membership on sports teams — enlarges chances of success in whatever field a graduate chooses to enter. Including the sciences. But if Stanford knows this, why shouldn't you? I don't mean that to be a rhetorical question.

Every year, Harvard, Yale, Princeton and other elites turn away thousands of applicants with perfect SAT scores and thousands with perfect 4.0 GPAs. Harvard turns down four out of every five valedictorians who apply. But shapely, well-dressed, physically vital candidates are given a substantial head start — as if elite college was some sort of eugenics project. Why did your high school never talk about this? Is college in part eugenically driven, part of the great Bionomics project begun in turn of the century America which led to the sterilization of tens of thousands of "biological defectives," and earned our academic fraternity medals from the Nazi government? What? You never heard of that? Didn't your school teach American history?

The most interesting part of this for me is that ugliness is hardly ever predestined by biology — you have to work to be ugly; it emerges as a byproduct of the "negative" education demanded by Adam Smith's publisher several hundred years ago.

Are you aware that the epidemic of diabetes in America, which now claims children down to the age of five, is caused directly by excessive immobility and a diet heavy in fats and sugars; are you aware that diabetes is our leading cause of amputations and blindness? In light of those facts, why would the largest middle-class occupation in America make its living imposing such unwholesome behaviors? If you hide from this question you might as well throw away this book.

Why are school people immune from lawsuits for physically damaging the incarcerated population? The answer has much to do with the supposed independence of the courts in the pragmatic era, inspired by Oliver Wendell Holmes. "Justice" was too crucial an element in 20th century management to take its demands seriously.

Irrelevance Revisited

To what degree are the curricula of schools and colleges beside the point, mere padding to fill long hours of confinement until the trapped lives, exhausted of their vitality, broken to the traces, can safely be released?

An MIT professor, Langdon Winner, provides an answer in his book, *Autonomous Technology,* which carries the ominous sub-title: *Technics Out-of-Control,* intimating what Lewis Lapham said openly in the Summer 2008 number of *Lapham's Quarterly:*"The arithmetic suggests we have no way of avoiding calamity..."

In the following citation from *Autonomous Technology,* Winner inventories deficiencies of the best schooled generations in American history. Be careful as you read not to fall into the trap schooling will have conditioned in your mind — that people are dumb by nature and we can't expect school to turn pigs into swans:

> Society is composed of persons who cannot design, build, repair, or even operate most of the devices upon which their lives depend...people are confronted with extraordinary events and functions that are literally unintelligible to them. They are unable to give an adequate explanation of man-made phenomena in their immediate experience. They are unable to form a coherent, rational picture of the whole... all persons do, and indeed must, accept a great number of things on faith...their way of understanding is basically religious, rather than scientific...The plight of members of the technological society can be compared to that of a newborn child...[but] Citizens of the modern age in this respect are less fortunate than children. They never escape fundamental bewilderment in the face of the complex world their senses report...

In a complex society, flexible people survive best, but school — think of the word itself — rewards rigid, miserable rule-followers. To be effective and remain independent we need to know how to find things out, how to manage our own learning, but the day prison model school discourages learning for its own sake. Actual learning leads directly to low test scores. Whatever education happens in school happens despite school, not because of it. Learning isn't the point of school, winning is; attention is never placed on quality of thought or performance, but on something entirely different; reaching the winner's circle.

Listen to a couple of random observations made long ago by two products of the best schooling, the first a famous writer, the second a successful stockbroker who ran away to the South Seas to become an influential painter:

> How infuriating not to know! All those years at Eton... Why didn't they teach me anything sensible?
>
> — Aldous Huxley

> By the second day I had exhausted my provisions. What to do? I had imagined that with money I would be able to find all that was necessary. I was deceived. Once beyond the threshold of the city... one must know how to climb the tall trees, how to go into the mountains in order to return weighed down with heavy booty. One must know how to catch fish, and how to dive to tear loose the shellfish... One must know how, one must be able to do things.
>
> — Paul Gauguin, *Noa Noa*

Neither Huxley nor Gauguin were taught anything useful by their school time; both found themselves frustrated in later life, imperfectly anchored in reality because of all the time wasted in school in low-grade abstractions memorized, which lacked any utility; administered in a climate of intimidation.

Seymour Papert (of the MIT Artificial Intelligency Laboratory) said in his book *Mindstorms* that *all learning can be learned "as the child learns to talk, painlessly, successfully, and without organized instruction.*

[emphasis added]...schools as we know them today will have no place in the future." Papert offered two possible destinies for institutional schooling — transformation "into something new" or "wither away and be replaced." In the decades since that was written, nearly three million homeschoolers have emerged and well over a million people drop out of school as of 2009. In urban schools it's an open secret that after lunch, classroom attendance is difficult to maintain and attention virtually impossible.

The Dark World of Compulsory Schooling

The minute you are willing to acknowledge how radically irrelevant school offerings actually are, the question of intent rears its disturbing head. Is this irrelevance an accident of incompetence? Is it possible the managers of institutional schooling don't know themselves what to do, but having inherited command of a dangerously unstable vessel, must sail it somehow to a destination unknown? For an army of local superintendents and principals this is surely true — the job is too good to abandon, its perks too rich to give up; they might like to change and adapt but the command/control structure won't allow any strong deviations from system logic.

Yet even having granted professional frontline confusion, the spectre of some darker intent at the level of policy won't go away. Schooling in the short and intermediate run is so unmistakably beneficial to some of the orders of society who possess power to plan for the whole that the possibility of these surrendering to the temptation to use institutional schooling for social engineering can't be dismissed. And once that filter is activated in your critical consciousness, evidence presents itself constantly that indeed this is so. Consider this excerpt from a speech delivered in 1940 to the Association for the Advancement of Science by the legendary political philosopher and journalist, Walter Lippmann:

> ...during the past forty or fifty years those who are responsible for education have progressively removed from the curriculum

> the Western culture which produced the modern democratic state...the schools and colleges have therefore been sending out into the world men who no longer understand the creative principle of the society in which they must live...deprived of their cultural tradition, the newly educated Western men no longer possess in the form and substance of their own minds and spirits and ideas, the premises, the rationale, the logic, the method, the values of the deposited wisdom which are the genius of the development of Western civilization...the prevailing education is destined, if it continues, to destroy Western civilization and is in fact destroying it. I realize quite well that this thesis constitutes a sweeping indictment of modern education. But I believe the indictment is justified and there is a prima facie case for entering this indictment.

The details, events, and dramatis personae of the project to set aside Western culture — and their motives — have been exhaustively explored by a major scholar from Georgetown University, Dr. Carroll Quigley, in a phenomenal work of syntheses published in 1966, entitled *Tragedy and Hope: A History of the World in Our Time*.

Tragedy and Hope was so profoundly eye-opening a treatise that its New York publisher destroyed the plates after the first printing and when that small edition (2000 copies) was gone, declined to reprint it, although thousands of backorders were at hand. Dr. Quigley was deceived with the story his book had met with public indifference. Since that moment, tens of thousands of bootleg copies have issued from wildcat presses, so a Google search will put a copy in your hands. One caution: some of the most recent printings may have been altered to omit certain key passages. It would be such a shame to come right to the gates of life-changing revelation and then fall into the clutches of the disinformation crowd yet again, that I strongly recommend you buy one of the older versions available on Amazon — or better yet, consult one of the first editions if you can find one in the rare book room of your public library, or the closed stacks of the local university library.

Quigley, incidentally, was President Clinton's personal tutor at Georgetown, and is mentioned with respect at the end of Clinton's acceptance speech for the Democratic Party presidential nomination. You needn't fear falling into the hands of some reckless conspiracy nut whose eyes glow in the dark. Do the work, I promise you'll never see our schools or our world the same way again.

Scientific Management? (No! No! No!)

The first goal of Scientific Management — the high level cult created by efficiency engineer Frederick Taylor and formalized in his book *Principles of Scientific Management* (1911), which became the driving force in American business, government, schooling, religion, social work, and much else — is perfect subordination. The concept of hierarchy is especially important in bureaucracies where the notion of productivity is always amorphous — there everything is secondary to subordination. Better the ship should be blown to pieces than allow a common sailor to give the orders because he knows more than the captain.

Subordination is a religious principle, like transubstantiation; it involves a ladder system of functional boxes into which employees are confined; as long as they remain as placed, surrendering volition, they become predictable: interdependent human resources to be utilized as needed by management.

Educated people, or people with principles, represent rogue elements in a scheme of scientific management; the former suspect because they have been trained to argue effectively and to think for themselves, the latter too inflexible in any area touching their morality to remain reliably dependent. At any moment they may announce," This is wrong. I won't do it." Overly creative people have similar deficiencies from a systems point of view.

Scientific management is always on guard against people who don't fit securely into boxes, whether because of too much competency, too much creativity, too much popularity, or what have you. Although often hired, it is with the understanding they must be kept on a short leash and regarded warily. The ideal hireling is reflexively obedient, cheerfully enthusiastic about following orders, ever eager to please. Training for this position begins in the first grade with the word, "don't."

In primary school, when all the endless possibilities of self-development and the varieties of good life should be explored, the principal element taken up is limitation, signaled by the word, "don't."

Don't run; don't talk; don't climb trees; don't play rough; don't talk unless you raise your hand; don't fidget; don't get out of your seat; don't stare out the window; don't take your shoes off; don't eat or drink in class; don't laugh; don't take too long; don't read ahead; don't go off the path; don't say 'I'm bored'; don't mix with older kids; don't complain; don't bring toys, etc. together with the implied don'ts: don't have your own ideas; don't show initiative; don't be independent; don't make your own choices; don't take responsibility for your own learning.

There are more don'ts than days in the calendar, a tattoo without end. This non-stop negativity, so reminiscent of William Playfair's prescription for schooling in Scotland, breaks many a spirit. The most enduring legacy of the DON'T drill is indifference to everything except narcotic anodynes like violence, rudeness, cruelty, alcohol, and actual drugs with which the negativity can be escaped.

How do I know? I spent 30 years in classrooms with nearly 4000 teenagers, many of whom I spoke with personally; another 20 in classrooms as a student myself, and 20 more studying the school business and talking about it all over the world.

A school trip permission form sent in September, 2005, to parents of eighth grade pupils at the Queen Elizabeth Junior and Senior High School in Calgary, Canada will give you a good idea how schools discourage direct experience among parents as well as kids, as an important component of the negativity program:

> POTENTIAL HAZARDS MAY INCLUDE BUT ARE NOT LIMITED TO THE FOLLOWING:
>
> **Bus travel to and from site:** Motion sickness, injury from other person's motion sickness, injury from being thrown during sudden massive negative or positive acceleration,

tripping hazard when entering or exiting vehicle or moving down the aisle, overheating during transit, objects coming through open windows, injury from student putting head or limbs out of window, injury caused by own or other student's inappropriate behavior.

Entire trip: slipping or tripping getting on or off the bus, slipping while climbing stairs or pathway on the trail, exposure to pollens, food, dust, or other materials that might induce allergic reaction, dehydration, exposure to environmental conditions including cold, damp, warm, dry, hot, and sunny, tripping on sidewalk or paved pathways, attack or injury from wild animals, food-borne organisms in own or other students' lunches, snacks, or drinks, electrical storms including lightning strikes, landslides on hills.

Viewing indoor exhibits at site: tripping hazard on stairs, bumping hazard from other viewers, pinching, hazard form doors, slipping hazard on wet floor or pavements, injury from collapsing exhibits.

Unless you sign off on this catalogue and hold the school harmless for its part in exposing your hothouse flower of a kid to these pitfalls which exist every minute of every day in normal ordinary lives, your kid can't go to the museum but must stay behind in school where these perils also exist, but from which the courts have lightened school culpability significantly.

And what psychological effect does this grisly enumeration carry, repeated as it is on every excursion outside school walls? Is it designed to add value to the adventurous risk-taking without which the mass of the young are doomed to become and remain clerks lifelong? Forgive my sarcasm.

Connections and Disconnections Revisited

Following the Prussian prescription of our first national school czar, William Torrey Harris — to alienate individual children from themselves in order to have their identities merge into a group identity — contemporary school planners treat children as categories: black, white, Hispanic, other; gifted and talented, special progress, mainstream, special education; rich, middle-class, poor, and with multiple subdivisions of each imaginable category, rather than as specific individuals with specific intellectual, social, psychological and physical needs.

The rhetoric of collectivization leads quickly to treating groups and sub-groups as averages. This makes managerial labor much easier, but guarantees bad results no matter how many resources are devoted to improving the lot of the group. As with the well-funded Head Start program out of Washington, whatever small gains show statistically dissipate with time. The logic of collectivization seeks to disconnect each child from his or her own unique constellation, particular circumstances, traditions, aspirations, past experiences, families, and to treat each as the representative of a type. By a process as inexorable as that with which the collapsing walls of a prison room force the prisoner toward a pit and death in Poe's story, *The Pit and the Pendulum*, a collectively viewed classroom must aim for the lowest common denominator — a fatal decision from the start.

When the mayor of New York City, an excellent manager in every other regard, was given control of the city schools in 2002 (heretofore in control of system bureaucrats and state-level politicians), instead of raising academic standards for all, he took bad advice and sought to deal with system-wide failure — particularly among students of color — by lowering the bar for everyone. Between 2002 and 2008 he increased dollar spending on schools 79 percent, he added 5000 teachers to the payroll (even though the attendance rolls had lost 60,000 students over this time) and the result as such things are measured was zero.

All the while the current approach, embedding each student in a personalized curriculum whose aim would be to multiply the number of connections — to ideas, to experiences, to other people — was ignored. It would be shocking if it was even considered.

The educated mind is the connected mind, connected to all manner of different human styles (not the sterile equivalencies of a classroom), connected to all sorts of complex experiences, some of them fraught with psychological and physical peril (not the barren experiences of school bells in a prison of measured time); connected to a dizzying profusion of intellectual ideas which interconnect with one another, and in time, set the pulses racing with the sheer transcendence possible in the human prospect — a feeling like no other and sufficient to be its own reward without the candy prison of praise, gold stars, or the promise of future reward.

Most of all, the educated mind is connected to itself. There is not a major philosopher of Western history since Socrates who didn't discover that knowing yourself is the foundation for everything else. To do that you must examine every influence which became a part of you, as Roman emperor Marcus Aurelius begins to do in the opening of his *Meditations*. Without self-knowledge you can hardly think of yourself as human at all. And yet we have the first National Commissioner of Education, right at the start of things, declaring that self-alienation is the goal of schooling.

School disconnects, as it was charged to do. It is Caesar's "divide and conquer" strategy brought to peak efficiency. Children are divided from their families, their traditions, their communities, their religions, their natural allies — other children — their interests and on ad infinitum. They are, as Walter Lippman deplored, disconnected from the entire Western intellectual tradition which gave societies the greatest gift of personal liberties they had ever seen, disconnected from the experiences of risk-taking and adventure in which the grand discoveries of history have been fashioned; young men and women emerge from school unable to do much of anything, as Langdon Winner testified.

The Talking Choo-Choo Syndrome

On the 19th of February, 2007, I testified for a bill before the Montana legislature—Rick Jore's HR404—to abolish compulsory school attendance. Just that simple act of trust in ordinary people would, by itself, I think, act over time to topple the house of cards erected in the 20th century to prevent education from spreading. Whatever the truth of that proposition, on the airplane back to New York I took up the task of critiquing a bit of curriculum created for a chain of private schools on the West Coast.

I had visited one of these schools near Los Angeles in the company of the curriculum director and in the brief time there was impressed by the good manners and easy-going civility of teacher-student relations, and by the spirit of good will which visibly attended student efforts to participate in their own education. But two things bothered me a little. The first was this: in a meeting of school officials and myself, to chat about school matters, several older students were asked to sit in and though the discussion bore exclusively on their own school lives, they had nothing to say and weren't encouraged to participate. When I was invited to ask some questions, I directed the first to the students in the room, "If you could change some things, say one thing about this school, what would it be?" I sensed a certain unease, even mild shock, among everyone there, including the students. What could kids possibly know, or care, about the management of their studies?!

Nobody actually said that, it was simply a feeling I had that, except ceremonially, kids were in one compartment, professional staff in another, administration and curriculum experts in a third. Thus the powerful energy which would have been released by connecting all these parts to exchange information and insights was lost.

The second thing that bothered me was that upon leaving, when I paused to examine a shelf of eighth grade textbooks, my eye hit on Homer's *Odyssey*, a book which along with Homer's *Iliad* had once provided the beating heart of classical Greek education. Committed to memory by many thousands, recited from memory, these tales of the Trojan War and its aftermath were no simple stories with which to kill time, but a series of particular moral dilemmas which in one form or another would afflict everyone in the course of a lifetime. Debating the proper course of action in these provided a rich mental diet.

I was delighted to find *The Odyssey* as a part of the eighth grade curriculum until I opened the cover to find it was a bowdlerized version — rewritten and simplified for 13 and 14-year-old California students from prosperous families. As if the "meaning" could be abstracted from the language and presented in a livelier fashion than Homer. One thing is certain: if Homer had written the version I was holding, nobody except an "A" student anxious for a good grade would have ever read the book to its end, and the only way it would have survived to bore a second generation of reader would have been as a textbook in a compulsory school scheme.

But I was on my way out the door and these people not only had a school infinitely superior to the Los Angeles standard, but they were intelligent, caring folks nobody would have been reluctant to entrust their children to, so I made a casual comment that kids had been reading the original for a couple thousand years without protest, and left to catch my plane. The curriculum director asked if I'd look over a new workbook they were putting together for the elementary division, as we drove to LAX, and I said I would.

At 35,000 feet I opened the book and found myself face to face with a talking choo-choo as my guide through the workbook. Although it's a bare 18 months later as I'm writing, the only detail of the text I can remember is the talking choo-choo. Everything else has faded; indeed, it faded as I read. Back home I wrote to the curriculum director at once:

> 26 February, 2007
>
> Dear Dave,
> All that follows bears on the talking choo-choo your book is built around. I'm going to be candid because I like you so much, and enjoyed our talks in the brief time we've known one another. The talking choo-choo of child development theory is only one form of a German disease which insinuated itelf into school development around the turn of the 20th century. The first invasion of this disease was in the

kindergarten movement of the 19th century, but that never took sufficiently to satisfy its managers, so inserting cartoons into children's heads instead of real world ideas became the vogue as part of a great project to artificially extend childhood and childishness. The project started in earnest at the beginning of the century and was acknowledged and even boasted about — by the dean of Teacher Education at Stanford University, who played a hand in its inception.

As a weapon of mass instruction it's superior in its destructive effect to all the others, the master weapon as it were. It's a principal cause of the intense and growing childishness of Americans in every social class, an indictment I hear from every corner of the world as I travel — and increasingly from domestic commentators, too.

I know this is a heavy trip to lay at the doorstep of your choo-choo, but since this is just me talking to you I wanted to bypass the public relations aspect of things and strike at what troubles me about every sequential curriculum — simple to complex—I've ever seen. It's a strategy which has traveled under many names throughout history as leadership groups have worked to make their ordinary populations manageable. The project was brought to its scientific pinnacle in the early decades of the 19th century in Prussia and exported all around the world in the last half of that century.

That's why I call it the German disease — the artificial extension of childhood. Make no mistake, it works. Once sufficiently infected with the virus the disease is progressive. Its victims become inadequate to the challenges of their existence without help, and that relative helplessness makes them manageable.

Remember, I'm using your talking choo-choo metaphorically, there are many ways to interdict the growth of competence, of clear thinking, of forceful purpose, and each is a talking choo-choo in different guise: think of slasher flicks, think of pornography, think of Big Macs or tabloid/network news — each is easy to take, each seemingly an inconsequential time-killer. But ah! The ensemble of them playing their mindless tunes — the Death of a Thousand Cuts!

The genius lies in setting up a perverse hunger which defies eradication later on as the victim struggles to grow up. This implanted need for simplifications in everything makes self-discipline difficult, and for most of us, only indifferently possible. We can't grow up after the disease has taken over — think of the blockbuster Hollywood films not in cartoon form, think of Peter Pan, Michael Jackson, Britney Spears shaving her head bald and sucking her thumb, think of the incessant commercial, "I don't want to grow up, I'm a Toys-R-Us kid! I read in the *L.A. times* that upscale mothers try to dress and act like their nine-year-old daughters, I read in *The Nation* that the level of economic understanding is so minimal, so primitive, that it's difficult to conduct a discussion on any level beyond fairytale simplification of things.

The formula for talking choo-choo social control is set down in Calvin's *Institutes* (1535), refined impressively in Spinoza's *Tractate* (1670), and brought to institutional life by Fichte in the second decade of the 19th century. Since then it's been off to the races. The dark side of the Welfare State midwifed by Beatrice Webb and the Fabian socialists is not its superficial purpose of being kind, but its intention of killing with kindness, and thus protecting the interests of the better people, non-violently. The talking choo-choo is the tip of the tip of the iceberg on which the damned are consigned to be frozen intellectually, psychologically, and socially.

And now for a different way to see talking choo choos from the customary perspective (besides my own, that is). Consider Miss Beatrix Potter, subject of a movie about her life in 2007 and a biography by St. Martin's Press. In 1912 at the pinnacle of her success she excoriated her publisher for being afraid to print her new book unaltered, a tale of the kidnapping and near death of a sack of baby rabbits.

"I am tired of making goody-goody books," she wrote, "You are a great deal too much afraid." Potter saw correctly that what set her apart from the general run of children's tale-tellers was that she employed an "attitude of mind" full of darkness, violence, unsentimentality, and realism — exactly in the qualities which human life displays and which must be confronted directly if one is ever to become master of oneself. Children understand this, both implicitly and explicitly, and unlike schooling, Potter speaks to the need to think about these things. Her work is tart and crisp, dwelling frequently on death.

In *The Tale of Benjamin Bunny*, an owl picks up a squirrel, "intending to skin him."

The Tale of Jemima Puddle Duck traffics in transcendental evil as the fox asks Jemima to pick out the seasonings in which she is to be cooked.

> Fee Fie Foe Fum
> I smell the blood of an Englishman
> Be he live or be he dead
> I'll grind his bones to make my bread

Nothing is more interesting to young children than evil, cruelty, and malice; they are cognizant of these things before they can speak with any fluency. The hypocrisy of sweet animal tales and images in a culture which murders animals wholesale and eats them with lip-smacking gusto is lost on most desensitized adults, but almost never lost on their children. And this ugly skew from reality is only one of many such contradictions our talking choo-choo culture traffics in wholesale.

The effect of these amoral exercises is severe on children, despite apologetics practiced by child development experts who justify the practice.

There are talking animals in Potter, but none are cute. "Thank goodness my education was neglected," Potter wrote, but what she meant was talking choo-choo schooling. Potter's learning was of a high standard: she read Homer in the best translations, spoke fluent

German, and wrote frequently that she did not like children. She despised those spirits ruined by theories inflicted upon them in long-term forced confinement, especially the ones who produced childish responses long after they had developed an inner life, because it was expected of them. The fact that children are still strongly attracted to Potter is a triumph of truth over the official illusions of institutional schooling.

Detach the Training Wheels!

According to *The New York Times* of December 15, 2006, Elena Delle Donne is the best female basketball player in the country, with "the potential to alter the game for women in the same way Michael Jordan did for men." She's off to a major college without it costing her a nickel and she is destined to make millions in endorsements. I'm telling you about her, however, because of something she did at age three without any thought of basketball.

She picked up a wrench and without any guidance detached the training wheels from her bike! At three she freed herself from the curse of childhood, that exquisitely German invention. Freed herself of its damaging assumptions about what is possible and what is not. Try to imagine the internal organization that requires in a three-year -old: the close observation of wrenches, structure, processes; the planning that had to take place inside this thousand day old creature to even conceive such a plan, let alone execute it. To ensure more Elenas, school would have to abandon the convenience of treating large groups in the aggregate — as "classes." Insist on classes and most Elenas will be ruined in the egg. Think of Branson, think of Ben Franklin or George Washington, think of Octavia Walker and David Farragut described elsewhere in this book.

When, as happens with some frequency, I'm asked by parents for a single suggestion for changing the relationship between them and their kids for the better, I don't hesitate to recommend this:

Don't think of them as kids. Childhood exists, but it's over long before we allow it to be. I'd start to worry if my kid were noticeably childish past the age of seven and if by twelve you aren't dealing with young men and women anxious to take their turn, disgusted with training wheels on anything, able to walkabout London, do hundred mile bike trips, and add enough value to the neighborhood that they have an independent income; if you don't see this, you're doing something seriously wrong.

Even at seven don't edit the truth out of things. If the family has an income kids need to know to the penny what it is and how it's spent. Assume they are human beings with the same basic nature and aptitudes that you have; what you have superior in terms of experience and mature understanding should be exchanged for their natural resilience, quick intelligence, imagination, fresh insight, and eagerness to become self-directing.

Don't buy into the calculated illusion of extended childhood. It's a great secret key to power — power for your kids if you turn the tables on their handlers. And adolescence is a total fraud, a pure concoction of social engineers barely a century old. It's a paradox, constantly threatening to solve itself as the young beat against the school jail in which we've confined them. Sometimes as I read obituaries — far and away the most valuable department in a good newspaper—I stumble across a new piece of evidence that what I've told you is true.

On the 18th of April, 2003, for instance, my newspaper carried the obit of the world's 101st richest man, John Latsis. If that name sounds vaguely familiar it's because his grandson Paris Latsis was for a brief time engaged to Paris Hilton, the celebrity heiress and beloved cut-up whose fornication video has been a staple of the American male imagination since its release to the world.

John Latsis' yacht had been a familiar sight in the harbors of the planet for a long time before his death, having been loaned to Prince Charles, President Bush, Marlon Brando, Colin Powell and many other awe-inspiring somebodies. But nothing inspires my own awe more than Mr. Latsis' personal story.

Born to a poor Greek family in a Greek fishing village, childhood was a luxury his family couldn't afford. He had no schooling to speak of and began work as a laborer at the age of twelve. Latsis was ambitious for something more, however; eventually he hooked on as deckhand on a rusty tramp freighter. After World War II, rusty freighters were a drag on the international freight market; almost valueless there were so many, built to haul war supplies and soldiers.

At the age of 28 this poor boy, Latsis, took his savings and all the money he could borrow and put a down payment on one of the rusty freighters. Over the next 30 years he parlayed that single ship into a mighty fleet. Without any prompting from business school mentors (of which he had none) he gradually branched out from shipping into construction, oil, banking and other enterprises. His growing sophistication was a natural by-product of being fully connected to the world of affairs.

Seventy-five years ago, schools routinely spoke of alternative roads to success like Latsis'; they don't do that anymore. Eighty percent of the young today — even more — are prepared (in theory at least) for "good jobs," as specialized employees of one sort or another. Attention is never focused on lives like that taken by John Latsis; who made it without benefit of any formal education at all.

Tania Aebi and George Meeghan

Twenty years ago in 1989 a teenage girl named Tania Aebi sailed into New York Harbor after two years at sea alone, having circumnavigated the world — the first woman in history known to have performed this remarkable feat. She has no background in seamanship, no particular calling or aptitude for it, and only a vague knowledge of navigation when she set out, having failed Celestial Navigation on the Coast Guard exam. No matter. She taught herself the subject on board her vessel. And sailed her way into adulthood, the record books, and history.

Tania had such difficulties at Brooklyn Tech High School that she gradually stopped attending, as you can discover by reading her book, *Maiden Voyage*; her father, disgusted with her rudeness and general demeanor, wanted her out of the house and offered to buy her a 26 foot boat if she would sail it around the world alone. As a way to spite him, she accepted the challenge, dropped out, and did it.

Thirty years ago, a poor young man from England conceived the idea of making the longest walk in human history. George Meeghan had no college degree, no specialized training, no state-of-the-art equipment, no money, and no schooling beyond the third grade — he was a lowly deckhand on a nondescript steamer headed for the tip of South America. Leaving the ship there he made his way to Tierra del Fuego, faced north, and started to walk. His entire kit was towed behind him in one of those flimsy shopping carts people take to the market to roll their purchases home. The wheels kept coming off. It was like a joke.

It took George Meeghan seven years to cross the Andes, negotiate dangerous mountain nations, cross the trackless Darien Gap, and enter the United States. Once in Texas he decided to make a side trip to see Washington, DC —on foot of course — then turned northwest to Point Barrow, Alaska, to complete the longest walk in human history. The bare outline I've given you doesn't do George's saga (or Tania's) justice. I urge you to read his book, *The Longest Walk*, to discover what unschooled human beings are capable of. Recently, George's young daughter, Ayumi, walked the entire length of Japan from south to north.

Two dropouts, two triumphs of the human spirit. No school on earth would dream of teaching what they learned, to write their own scripts, to be self-sufficient and purposeful. The longest walk in human history (check the *Guinness Book* for George), the longest solo sail (check the *Guinness Book* for Tania)—if two young people without much help or special equipment could do this in the 1970s and 1980s on sheer will power, can you ever believe again the hypothetical academic hypotheses of human migration? If Tania and George did it with nothing, then anonymous others have done it before, too. "Academic" once referred to Akademos, the garden where Plato taught; it was a term of great respect for nearly two millennia, but by the late 19th century, it had come to mean "of slight human interest"; irrelevant.

Now contrast the lives of Tania and George with the lives of 25,000 intensely schooled young people who work in Washington, D.C. and let their hair down on weekends in Dewey Beach, Delaware:

> Dewey Beach, Delaware, July 5, 2001 — In *Corinthians*, Paul preaches that adults put away childish things. Clearly the apostle never summered in this mile-long stretch of beachtown. It is Friday afternoon, and 25,000 single professionals...are pouring into this village of 500 for their weekly ritual of regression...lobbyists, House and Senate aides, computer network developers and management consultants, ranging in age from 23-37. There will be a $420 bar tab at the Starboard tonight — A Saturday afternoon sexual escapade will occur in plain view of neighbors. A punch will be thrown on the dance floor... [this] ritual of hard-working singles shedding power suits for beachhouse escapism each Friday is in full swing.
>
> — *USA TODAY*

The Trapped Flea Principle

What accounts for the eerie inhuman passivity of school children toward matters the grown-up world has traditionally considered important? And the even weirder seeming indifference poor children display toward their ominous and onrushing futures? I had theories about this as a teacher, but never one I actually believed until an 11-year-old Taiwanese immigrant boy named Andrew Hsu explained how you break the spirit of fleas so they can be trained. His explanation was printed in a recognition ceremony in which Andrew and I were to receive the same foundation award. For me the honor paled in comparison to what I learned from Andrew that day.

In the first place, he was fresh from winning the Washington State Science and Engineering Fair, for his sequencing of a gene held in common between man and mouse: COL201A. At 11, Andrew was a champion swimmer with many trophies. He spoke Chinese, champion swimmer with many trophies. He spoke Chinese, French, and English, all fluently. He worked in his spare time as an assistant on professional documentary films. And he was homeschooled.

When asked to describe the most important lesson of his life, the one which held the most influence over his choices, he said it was a story told to him by his father about the method used to train fleas to swing on trapezes, drive little chariots, (or pull them) and all the other wonderful things fleas learned to do to amuse kings and courts in world history. The story his father told goes like this:

If you put fleas in a shallow container they jump out. But if you put a lid on the container for just a short time, they hit the lid trying to escape and learn quickly not to jump so high. They give up their quest for freedom. After the lid is removed, the fleas remain imprisoned by their own self-policing. So it is with life. Most of us let our own fears or the impositions of others imprison us in a world of low expectations.

Reading that, my whole life as a schoolteacher flashed before my eyes. I had been hired to be the lid on the petri dish which the kids would butt their heads trying to follow their own path until one day, exhausted, they would quit trying. At that point they would be fit subjects to be trained.

How to Drive a Horse Slightly Insane

The time we spend trapped in schooling and its humbug renders most of us passive, incompletely human, unable to function as sovereign spirits. But other tools exist to clip our wings, just to be safe. Those who break out of the school doors or hang out in bathrooms and stairwells aren't the biggest problem — after all, where can they run? The biggest danger to the social order comes from those who retreat into the secret recesses of their inner lives where no snoop can penetrate.

For this hard core contingent, an insight of horse breeders provides another strategy. By taking known dangers to a horse's sanity, things to be avoided if you want your thoroughbred to be productive, and instead of avoiding them you *impose* these conditions, it's possible to drive young people to work against their own best interests, seeking connections, and send them deep into the prison of self to play "Dungeons and Dragons," computer games, or endlessly surf the Web instead of taking risks or learning how to be effective.

Some years back I saw with some surprise my school experience mirrored in the pages of a highly specialized journal, a publication of the Equine Mental Health Association. The relevant article was paper-clipped and mailed from Frankfurt, Kentucky, by a Mr. and Mrs. Howard, horse enthusiasts like my wife, Janet. It considers damage done to quality horseflesh when the scope of their daily experience is over-simplified:

Tick off the conditions which cause a horse to go slightly crazy as you read and compare them to the familiar discipline of an average school:

> ...Keep them predominantly idle, keep them apart from other horses, and you will create an animal that interacts with the world in ways clearly un-natural...timid, crazy, undependable, bolting, bucking, avoidant, shying, etc. Keep a horse from accessing the wisdom of the herd and the wisdom of its own nature and you get a horse that doesn't know where it belongs in the world. Under such conditions well-bred horses with tremendous potentials end up living their lives as...consumers instead of contributors.

Consumers rather than contributors. Of course that's the point, which you already understand if you've followed the meandering argument of my book closely — mass-market corporate capitalism and the financial capitalism which has been replacing it for some time, both need consumers who define the value of their lives by consumption; both understand that only a small fraction of people need to know how to produce — and anything beyond that small fraction is a deadly poison to the system because the spectre of overproduction will frighten capital into hiding.

Overproduction has to be stopped is the policy belief. Schools are the principal factory in which that is done; consumption on the other hand has to be enhanced — and no condition stimulates consumption like boredom, especially when the imagination and the inner life have been paralyzed by endless memory drills, the synthetic crises of continual testing, and a thorough conditioning in rewards and punishments, the game of winners and losers. Do people actually think this way? If you ask me that question, I'd have to reply with some sorrow: Yes.

The Cauldron of Broken Time

When time is tightly scheduled, we are compelled to attend more to the appearances of attention and concern than to the reality of those qualities; without uninterrupted time you haven't a prayer of synthesizing the fact bits thrown at you. It's possible to memorize the official meaning of those bits, but in the time available no possibility remains of arriving at your own careful conclusions. After years of study, we know that uninterrupted sleep time is essential for precision in thought, but as Claire Wolfe, a West-Coast writer once taught me, uninterrupted waking time is similarly essential. When you can't concentrate, it's hard to make sense of things. Rather than persist in trying, it's easier just to quit.

The destruction of uninterrupted time is a major weapon of mass instruction. Schools are a rat's maze of frantic activity,: bells, loudspeakers, messengers pounding on classroom doors, shrieks from the playground, official visitors, unofficial visitors, toilet interruptions coming and going, catcalls, bullyings and flirtings — you never know when the next interruption will appear. Try to reckon the psychological effect of being plunged into a cauldron of broken time, in Miss Wolfe's phrase, again and again for 12 years (in the student's case) and even longer in the teacher's.

Personal time is the only time we have in which to build theories, test hypotheses of our own, and speculate how the bits of information our senses gather might be connected. Time allows us to add quality to our undertakings. It took only one knock at the door to ruin Coleridge's mighty poem Kubla Khan. I wasn't that sensitive as a classroom teacher, but after three interruptions — and my years in harness averaged seven per class hour — my brains were so scrambled I faked the rest of the lesson.

The End

I hope this has been enough to continue weapon-hunting on your own. Writing this has made me so sad and angry. I can't continue.

"Weapons of Mass Instruction" was first delivered, in shorter form, as the keynote speech for South Korea's National Education Convention, held at the University of Seoul in 2007.

8

What is Education?

Kant's Questions and the Epic of Europe

The great German philosopher Immanuel Kant, posed four questions he believed were at the heart of any educational quest:

What can I know?

What may I hope?

What ought I to do?

What is Man?

It's surely one of the great ironies of modern life that Germany, a national culture which revered Kant as the ultimate *übermensch*, created a form of youth training which virtually extinguished philosophical curiosity at home, and aggressively exported its system throughout the world in the nineteenth and twentieth centuries. You need only Google Horace Mann's famous "Seventh Letter to the Boston School Committee" to dispel any lingering illusions that American compulsory schooling is a home-grown product, or that it aims to transmit "basic skills" as those are generally thought to be. At root, it is German.

All of Kant's questions must be grappled with before a useful curriculum can be set up to reach the ends you wish. But if you duck this work, or are tricked into ceding it to an official establishment of specialists (or coerced into doing the same thing), it shouldn't surprise you to find yourself and your children broken on the wheel of somebody else's convenience, someone else's priorities.

You'll never come close to the exalted condition education can offer, where money and fame don't matter very much, as long as you remain content to memorize somebody else's definition of the thing, but reflecting seriously on what someone else says about it isn't worthless. It can bring you closer to your own truth — as Supreme Court Justice Potter Stewart said about pornography, "I can't define it, but I know it, when I see it." With that in mind, I'm going to offer you no comprehensive definition, but three "probes" into the mystery: one from an unusually acute travel writer named James Salter; one from a statement I gave to a Senate committee seventeen years ago; and one from a free verse scribbled on a legal pad while I was wrestling with the idea for a letter I intended to send to my granddaughter, Kristina, which you'll find as Chapter Nine in this book.

James Salter was looking for a way to capture in words the admiration he felt for the continent of Europe and its history. He began by saying that Europe helps to clarify Kant's questions:

> The thing it finally gave me was education, not the lessons of school but something more elevated, a view of how to endure: how to have leisure, love, food, and conversation, how to look at nakedness, architecture, streets, all new and seeking to be thought of in a different way. In Europe the shadow of history falls upon you and, knowing none of it, you realize suddenly how small you are. To know nothing is to have done nothing. To remember only yourself is like worshipping a dust mote. Europe is on the order of an immense and unfathomable classroom, beyond catalogue or description.

Confronted with the mighty epic of Europe and its inexhaustible bounty, Salter is able to see how far "the lessons of school" are from education. Look around you at America, as he did Europe: did your own schooling teach you how we got this way?

The next two offerings are my own. On October 23, 1991, I got an invitation to give testimony to the US Senate Committee on Labor and Human Relations. The subject: speculation what schools in the year 2000 were going to look like. Although I've polished prose, grammar, and syntax a little to spare myself embarrassment that an old English teacher would write so sloppily, the argument remains as I delivered it. And the reader will note that the future, as I foresaw it a decade down the line, happened right on schedule. Senator Ted Kennedy of Massachusetts was the committee chair:

Senator Kennedy, distinguished committee members, guests: what we should most fear is that school in 2000 will look exactly like school in 1990. School in 1990 is almost exactly like school was in 1890. Keep in mind, however, that if we moved back almost another hundred years, to 1790, the echoes would vanish.

In 1790 it was still possible to become educated in America because school didn't preempt all the time of the young, nor did it act as a leech upon family life then; it didn't impose servile habits on the growing up time; it didn't indoctrinate young minds with a burden of too many pre-thought thoughts.

It was still possible to *take* an education in 1790 because too many people weren't around pretending to *give* you one, forcing you to accept what they offered under penalty of law. In your own Massachusetts, Senator, more citizens were literate under a system where schooling was voluntary and of short duration, than ever they have been under the long-term compulsion scheme in place right now.

Whether it will ever again be possible to take an education easily, in Massachusetts or any other state, will depend upon political decisions made by those — like yourselves — who hold power in trust for the rest of us. I mean no disrespect, only to signal my personal sadness when I say I don't think those decisions will be made. My reasons for pessimism stem from knowing that failure is built into our political system because it forces our political leadership to depend for its election on the same financial interests which profit from schools staying the way they already are. Schools are a most lucrative source of contracts and an enormous jobs project with sinecures for friends and relatives of your campaign donors. Don't chalk that up to cynicism: unless you acknowledge why your hands are tied in regard to school change, you're certain to make the same mistakes year after year in counterfeit reforms.

Change isn't likely to be possible from any political center for the same reason, but it can come from defiant personal decisions made by simple men and women who won't stand still for their kids being outraged any more — like the revolution of homeschoolers taking place nationwide. This system has had a century to prove itself, that's enough. It didn't work at the start except in house-generated fairy tales; it doesn't work today, and it won't work better in the future.

But if we can pry the boot of the political state off our necks, by the year 2000 here's what might begin to emerge. First we'd have a long, loud national, regional, and local debate whose purpose would be to establish the range of acceptable definitions of an educated person.

Professional pedagogy has never done that except in the airiest generalizations because it knows better than to have its hands tied to commitments it can't deliver. At the most arrogant end of the institutional spectrum we have public enemies like James Bryant Conant, the WWI poison gas specialist and longtime president of Harvard, who announced in 1959 that education is "whatever a school delivers." Dr. Conant was annoyed that any mere citizen might think he had the right to question decisions made by experts like himself. What he demanded for himself, in essence, was the right to say, "Education is whatever I say it is."

But a public definition of the goals of mental and character training can't be avoided. If we the people don't agree on ends there is no way on earth to make beginnings — would you set out by car on a 12-year journey whose destination was "out there somewhere"?

The principal target of school time at present, a target many self-satisfied men and women congratulate themselves upon knowing, is the production of high standardized test scores — which correlate with almost nothing of value. Every president of the United States since such testing was launched has had a mediocre to poor standardized test score; the same is more true than not among corporate executives. If the scores had any meaning wouldn't they be a common piece of data demanded by consumers? Would you bet on a horse without consulting its past performance charts reduced to mathematical data? Yet you are compelled to bet on schoolteachers, principals, superintendents, college professors, etc. every day without being given access to this "valuable" information. What kind of lunacy is that? High standards and standardization are two very different things but you have been deliberately led by the rules of Newspeak to regard them as the same, just as you've been conditioned to think of education and schooling in the same breath.

The long, loud, angry national debate I'm calling for, Senator, would settle school's side of the bargain by producing a list of valuable human competencies schools would guarantee to enhance — or lose their ability to command attendance with the police power of the state.

That said, let me give you my own list:

- Educated people are seldom at a loss what to do with time; being alone is often a blessing to the educated because they like their own company. Time doesn't hang heavily on their hands.
- Educated people can form healthy attachments anywhere because they understand the dynamics of relationships.
- Educated people are aware of, accept, and understand the significance of their own mortality and each of its seasons. They learn from each moment, they gain insight all their ages, even to their last minutes on earth.
- Educated people possess a hard-won personal blueprint of value. They accept no prepackaged marching orders without passing them through the test of critical review. But they are also aware of a larger, human community and its values, are knowledgeable about values in different cultures.
- Educated men and women enjoy power to create new things, new ideas and new experiences; the educated discover truth for

themselves through the rules of evidence, not by memorizing opinions of others.

- Educated people detect other people's needs and in moving to meet those needs earn a living. But unlike the ignorant, the educated never become overly dependent on material wealth for happiness, recognizing that the most valuable goods — love, curiosity, reverence, and empathy — can be had without cost.
- Educated people actively seek variety and know how to master it sufficiently for pleasure and enlightenment. Yet they are aware, too, that without a home of their own and home responsibilities variety is hollow, experience superficial.
- The curriculum to become educated is drawn from great life passages which have united generations from the beginning of time. First is the mystery of birth and the mysterious emergence of self. To explore self requires intimate knowledge of one's parents and ancestors — and of the specific cultures which helped form them. The local cultures, that is, much more than the abstract entities we call political states. Who am I? Where are my limits? What are my possibilities? What range do the strange selves about me display? Exploring these things are like crucial appointments an educated person must keep; without honoring these only incomplete adulthood results.
- The physical world near and far must be thoroughly examined, analyzed, tested. This is work which can't adequately be done in confinement or through blackboard abstractions. When compulsion-schooling steals time needed for this work the damage is great. There is a time and place in life's sequence when these appointments must be kept; too-long delayed and opportunity is lost forever.
- The complex possibilities of association must be encountered and wrestled with — it won't work to merely talk about these, or see TV shows. They include family relationships, friendships, companionships, comradeship, love, hate, community, networking and more. Each has strengths and dangers inherent in the form.

Not to practice each early on is to risk becoming emotionally crippled. But confinement schooling is designed to socialize children into networks — the very weakest and least reliable of all human associations. Networks are certain to betray your trust if relied upon excessively.

- Another major theme which takes attention in the educated mind is a thoughtful approach to vocation — how does one contribute to the common good and at the same time earn a living? Then we meet the theme of "growing up" as a vocation of its own. How is that distinct from being a child? What complex of obligations accepted does growing up entail, acceptance of which brings maturity and independence?
- And we can't leave out a very close study of Death, the last act of the dramatic cycle begun by the mystery of Birth. Without clear awareness of the short arc of a life, nothing means very much. If we lived forever, no choice would ever be significant because endless time would be available to choose again and again. Time is strictly finite. Every choice precludes another, that's the reality which vests existence with meaning. We need to realize that the dying owe the oncoming generations a world at least as good as the one they experienced while fully alive; if possible a better one.

Give Up the Cathedral

Any school which hopes to educate must surrender the safety of the walled compound; must surrender the security of employing a priesthood certified for docility and political correctness; must give up the papacy of the political state and its economic partners. In the short run this conveys advantage (to the controlling parties), but over time it bleeds the commonwealth of its vitality — as it bled the once powerful Soviet Union — and leaches from the economy its ability to adapt to changing circumstances. In grabbing for short term economic advantage, schools are being charged with preventing education — the signs of decay because of that proscription are everywhere. If walled compound schooling were ended, corrupt relationships with universities, textbook publishers, building contractors, bus companies, and other protected suppliers who thrive on a mass captive audience would wither quickly.

Our new school, if it ever happened, would eliminate centralized testing because of what these rituals do in ranking children by abstract measures. They have little connection with developing mental powers, or the character traits of good citizens. Tests restrict the very development we claim to be seeking.

Our new school would eliminate testing for other reasons, too, finally accepting what experience clearly demonstrates — testing is a poor predictor: Mass testing institutionalizes dishonesty; it belongs to predatory cultures, not dynamic republics. Let testing return to China and the Manchu dynasty which spawned it. Because testing correlates with nothing very real, it mis-identifies winners and losers in a reckless fashion. Among its many unfortunate by-products is that testing targets problems for attention which aren't problems at all. Take the problem of poor reading, a self-correcting deficiency when the game-board can be set up differently. Once mis-identified by test scores, however, the creation of bureaucracy to "solve" the non-problem can seem a rational thing to do. I use reading as the emblem of this wasteful craziness because it may be the principal motor driving forced schooling.

To learn to read and to like it takes about thirty contact hours under the right circumstances, sometimes a few more, sometimes a few less. It's a fairly easy skill for anyone to pick up if good reasons to do so are provided. Exhortation isn't sufficient, however, nor intimidation, humiliation, or the confusion of a classroom full of strangers. The only way you can stop a child from learning to read and liking it — in the densely verbal culture which surrounds us all with printed language anywhere we turn — is to teach it the way we teach it.

You should begin with the attitude that *nothing is wrong* in the natural variation which finds one child reading at five and another at twelve. By the time both are fifteen nobody can tell which one learned to read first. The real trouble isn't with the kid, it's that you can't run schools the way I just described. The pedagogical apparatus which compels age-graded five-year-olds to be ranked according to ability to respond "correctly" to a teacher's urgencies gives rise to our familiar reading pathologies. By the time a seemingly slow reader approaches adulthood, he or she will display indifference to reading, or hatred of it, because of our methods.

So far our new school has dropped use of a walled compound. It occurs everywhere: on farms, in ships, in private homes, in churches, offices, on hillsides in the grass, and in rooms of a thousand complexions. It has decertified schoolteaching completely so that anyone with a skill to transmit can touch those who want to learn that skill. The Internet makes this transformation simple. All we lack at present is will to bring it about against the opposition of those who benefit from things as they are. What makes achieving that will particularly difficult is that the opponents to change are all too frequently our relatives or ourselves.

This new school we're creating puts money to purchase outside educational help back in the hands of taxpayers. That will break the monopoly on the training of youth and restore an open system of learning from everywhere we enjoyed from colonial times to the end of the Civil War. Monopolies suppress initiative, make poor use of feedback from customers who have nowhere else to go, and generate an aversion to truth.

Our new school has flexible time commitments operating in flexible spaces with flexible study options and flexible sequencing. It has these things not because of any momentary fashion, but because the range of human variety demands it.

We will discard standardized testing entirely but not standards of high quality. Standardization cripples imagination and imagination has always been the real driving engine of our powerful economy. The rankings these tests generate argue quite dishonestly that they correlate tightly with real-world excellence, yet they do nothing of the sort. The only way these judgments, based upon number-magic, can be made to seem functional is to rig the game in advance. That is to say if you only license people with high test scores, regardless of actual merit in designing buildings, removing tonsils, or teaching school, then you create a world of self-fulfilling prophecy in regard to test scores.

Any type of change which will produce new value for our society through schooling will involve less school time, less school personnel, less store-bought materials, less interference in the natural processes of learning. Any school reform that will work, academically and behaviorally, will cost much less money than we are currently spending. It will involve gradual merging of schooling with community life, a de-professionalization of the learning enterprise.

That's why positive change directed from the top isn't likely to happen: it would require political courage from men and women who benefit greatly from the existence of mass schooling and the jobs and contracts it commands. It's a dilemma worthy of Solomon, one which virtually demands that reform come from the bottom, not the top; from millions of acts of productive sabotage on the part of parents and students, and yes — from teachers like myself. We must behave like noble termites, tunneling the current structure until it dissolves of its own dead weight: we must encourage schoolpeople to sabotage the system while pretending not to.

I know how odd this all sounds: first I tell you reading, writing, and arithmetic are easy to learn as long as they aren't taught systematically, and now I tell you that the very "comprehensive" school institution which Harvard called for in the 1950s is ruining our children, not helping them. I know you've been told by experts that the complicated world of today requires more school time, longer school days, longer years, more testing, more labeling.

Well Senators, you've been bamboozled, and I hope your own experience will confirm that by a little reflection. How do you think millions of Americans learned to be literate on desktop computers, and all the rest of the paraphernalia of the information society. Not at school that's for sure.

For heaven's sake, my own school, in the rich west side neighborhood of Manhattan, doesn't even have a clock on the wall! Or a telephone, a fax machine, or a word processor accessible to teachers or students. How then did we learn to use computer? By struggle, struggling with directions translated from Japanese, by whining to friends, by watching others, by networking, by purchasing free-market lessons, reading books, pushing ourselves. We learned to compute the same way we learned to drive — without much professional help.

Isn't it obvious a lot of people who are making good use of computers right now would have failed computer class in school? Many would have been too embarrassed, too scared, too angry and confused in a school setting to really learn. We don't learn anything else there very well, why would computers be any different?

In another twenty years when every school is computerized, can't you predict already schools claiming that without school training, we never could have made a transition to the information age? You and I will know that isn't so, won't we?

Draw a parallel with driving. It's a dangerous ballet of hand/eye/foot coordination while simultaneously providing the intellectual challenge of constant calculation, strategy, and life and death split-second choices. Notice that everyone who does this actually learns to do it on their own. Yet in spite of mortal risk, almost everyone who doesn't drink while doing it does it OK. Indeed, our commercial civilization, spread out as it is, would be hurt badly if they didn't. That's why we don't demand drivers be schooled, only that they be competent.

And think of this: none of these drivers is graded, they pass or they fail the driving test; if they fail they take it a second or third or tenth time until they pass. Almost everyone eventually passes. Now regard the potential effect of this "success for all" system on your own life. Your safety has deliberately been placed in the hands of millions of unknown motorists whenever you drive, even when you walk on public streets. At any given moment, you don't know whether the blonde sailing by in her white Corvette was on the Dean's List as a driver, or whether she barely passed on the tenth try by flirting with the instructor. Shouldn't you be terrified of all this ignorance with so much power to snuff out your life or cripple you?

Shouldn't motorists have to mount illuminated signs indicating the grade of driver they are? You couldn't argue against such an initiative on reasonable grounds given the low opinion of humanity reflected in our politics, our media, and our pedagogy. It makes sense, yet the idea is utterly ridiculous. We expect one another, whatever our grades or test scores, to use good judgement in driving and for the most part, we aren't disappointed.

Grades and test scores are a terrible measure of quality. The sooner we recognize that in planning, the sooner we'll reach better ways to help our young. After teaching for 30 years, and winning awards doing it, I can say flatly what everyone knows in their gut — the best readers, the best writers, the best mathematicians, the best scientists are almost never people who got the best grades. You all sought the position of leader, Senators, and I'm asking you to face the implications of that squarely — find the courage to flaunt the financial interests which use schooling as a cash cow.

If you can't do that, all the Senate committees in the world won't give American students a better deal in school.

A Free Verse for Kristina

Whatever education is
it should make a girl unique
not a servant
It should give her courage
to tackle the big challenges, to find principles which
will serve as a guide on the road ahead,
Make her strong in the
presence of evil,
Let her love her fate whatever it is,
above everything, it should lead her to discover
what really matters:
How to live and how to die.

— John Taylor Gatto

9

A Letter to My Granddaughter About Dartmouth

Family Matters

Hello Kid,

On the wall as I type this is a newspaper photo of you holding up the tickets you got riding your bike on Fifth Avenue in defiance of a city ban. You're grinning. So am I. I don't know if Janet and I are prouder of you for that, or for being captain of a national champion debating team, or for going to court to change your name from Gudrun to Kristina. A tie I think. Your contrarian ancestors are smiling, too.

You come from a long line of boat-rockers, it must be in the DNA. Your granny Janet's clan was outlawed by the British crown. Your great-great-granny from Glenorchy wore a top hat. And the immortal outlaw Rob Roy called your clan his own.

Janet and I were married in the famous Buddhist Temple near Columbia on Riverside Drive, the one with the bronze Buddha statue outside which sat at ground zero where the atomic bomb exploded in Hiroshima in 1945, yet remained undamaged. She was under 18 and in those days the law said marriage with a girl that young had to happen in a church or other house of worship, not at City Hall. We were both unemployed, both far from home, and both broke so we couldn't afford what the Catholics, Protestants, or Jews charged (we tried them all), but the Buddhists said to come on over, they would do it for free. Janet was pregnant with your mother at the time.

After we got hitched your grandmother got a job, but she was fired in two weeks because she tried to organize a union at her non-union workplace. I got a job on Madison Avenue as an office assistant, but got fired, too, because I couldn't use a three-hole punch correctly and ruined copies of an agency presentation scheduled to be distributed that afternoon.

On the Italian/German side, your great great grandfather Giovanni, for whom I'm named, came from the family which owned the title, "Lords of the Straits of Messina" in the 17th century. He was hounded out of Italy at the beginning of the twentieth century for being a Presbyterian, a rabble-rousing journalist, and a Freemason in the days when none of those things were looked upon kindly in Italy. Your great great grandmother, Lucrezia, who he married, lost her inheritance (a bergamot plantation near Reggio) and her title (she was a comtessa) for marrying him. They left Italy, came to Pittsburgh, and thrived for a while. Andrew Mellon, the banker, personally hired him to oversee the Foreign Exchange division of the Mellon Bank in a time when immigrants swarmed to the Steel City for work in the mines and mills. The Gattos were Caruso's hosts when the great tenor came to town.

But prosperity didn't last. Giovanni died at 49, from an excess of champagne, caviar, and high living. When he passed on he was Grand Venerable of the Masonic Order for the state of Pennsylvania. Eighty-eight black limousines came from all over to his funeral, but Lucrezia buried him in an unmarked grave in Allegheny Cemetery in Pittsburgh. His crime? Moving his mistress Amalia into the family home and pretending she was the maid! Your mother has Lucrezia's diamond wristwatch.

Your great-grandfather, Harry Taylor Zimmer, town printer for the river town of Monongahela and travelling circus owner was a rabid

Republican even though everyone in town was a Democrat. He ran for mayor every few years, printing incredibly violent attacks on his opponents. In 1948, the local congressman came to our home to beg my mother to have old Harry withdraw his support for the congressman's re-election. He told mother he would lose in a landslide if people found out Zimmer was backing him.

I remember vividly the days of WWII when your great granddad would stand in the middle of Main and Second calling loudly for German victory! That made the daily walk up Second Street Hill to the Waverly School every morning with a dozen kids livelier than I care to remember. The only thing that saved me from many a beating was that everyone knew Bud Zimmer, Harry's magnificent son, the toughest man in town and a demon with his fists, was my uncle. Nobody cared to be on Bud's bad side.

Bud went on to be a field officer at the Battle of the Bulge, driven around by his aide in the jeep "Monongahela" which appeared in several newsreels of the front lines to great cheering by locals. One of the men who served under Bud turned out to be industrial giant, Al Rockwell. Mr. Rockwell bestowed the managership of his vast plant near Cincinnati on Bud even though my uncle lacked any college training.

Well, enough of family. You're a chip off the old block alright, Kristina.

Dartmouth College

I'm not writing to reminisce about your ancestors, but because you turned 17 in March and I heard you were up to White River Junction to interview for early admission at Dartmouth. Just like that, your childhood is over.

Bud gave me some good advice when I was 17 with a head that was swimming with dreams of Ivy League glory. He said to take a few years off and work until I understood myself better. It was great advice, but I didn't take it (wish now I had), and I suspect it would be hopeless to pass on to you, too, so I won't. But I do want you to think long and hard about going to Dartmouth or to any school famous for its power to confer social privilege on you. It's an illusion, they can't, and even if they could, such a state turns your life into a prison, with each hour of the day and each association predestined.

Don't trust what your high school, or your friends, have to say about this — the latter have been brainwashed just as you have and the former doesn't work in your best interests but in the interests of a system you don't understand. Your four years at a special high school will have infused you with the essential gospel of our command economy — that college is the foundation of a successful life and that only elite colleges like Dartmouth possess the secrets you need. Never mind that nobody could actually tell you specifically what happens at those places, in those seats, to transform you. It must be taken on faith like the virgin birth.

As you await the college's fateful decision you'll hear friends say that if they don't get the fat acceptance envelope to a prestige school they will kill themselves. Every year a few desperate souls do just that. I remember back in the early 1950s when Duke turned me down I was ready to enlist in the Army until my second choice, Cornell, opened its heart and took me in. As for Pitt or Penn State where the common herd grazed, it was unthinkable for a snob like myself to contemplate. Such was the malignant influence of the country club set over my judgement.

Feelings like this are common now in our country, a clear sign our once brilliant uniqueness grounded in hard-nosed egalitarianism is dead. The philosophy abroad in American schools these days was best rendered by George Orwell in *Animal Farm* as a belief among managerial pigs that although all animals, of course, are equal, some animals are more equal than others.

If you feel that way, even a little bit, get rid of it as you would a tumor. It's a moral cancer and it will eat you alive if you accept it. The best part of America, our promise that everyone who tries will have a turn, is on life support because of the spread of this ugly stain. Where you go to college, or even if you go at all, only makes a difference if you believe the spell which has been put on you. Is it money you want? In an hour from where you live I could take you to a common hot dog vendor who makes more of that than the mayor of New York and the president of the United States combined. Is it being of real use to society? Become a pet sitter so that people can take a vacation without abusing their critters. Like voodoo, where you go to college — or if you go at all — is only a real question in minds bewildered by illusion.

That's not to say education doesn't matter. It does. You need finely tuned critical judgement to defend yourself in the dangerous house of mirrors America has become. It's just that college won't give you education. Only you can do that.

Be patient a little longer with an old fellow and let me tell you what kind of schooling I think Dartmouth represents and then what kind I think you need. You will learn how to game the system at Dartmouth, I won't try to deny that, and you'll learn how to conceal your pain and confusion. You'll learn to think how and what the boss wants you to think, how to dress as the boss wants you to dress, and how to value what the boss wants you to value. And you'll learn to believe that all those things were your own idea. It's very subtle, Dartmouth's teaching; you won't even realize it's happening.

The first clue to the change will be when you suddenly realize how uncomfortable your own parents make you feel. How you wish they would butt out of your life.

Dartmouth is all about contrived problems, nothing real. The "case study" method is big there, part of a system which deludes its followers into thinking that application can be learned by simulation. A little of that doesn't hurt, but a lot is worse than worthless: It fills you with false confidence that complex problems are fully amenable to method — like repairing machinery is — but when you try to fit human beings into the abstract simplifications of method you discover they have to be forced to obey the theory. And sometimes they force back. Iraq, Afganistan, Sudan, all gifts of think-tank methodology, and all impervious to solution by method.

At 17 you want a way to measure the advance of our own education. I'll toss you eight yardsticks and you tell me where you are at the moment on the metrics of real education:

Grandpa John's Real Learning Index

1. **Self-knowledge:** This is the biggest prize of all. Without it you are lost and will flounder again and again through life. By now you should have introspected enough to know your own character: its proclivities, strengths, weaknesses, blessings, curses. How much assistance has your high school given you to accomplish this?
2. **Observation:** Your powers of observation in any situation should be razor sharp; at will you should be able to function like an objective camera/tape recorder sucking in accurate data for later analysis. Can you "read" the primary documents and images from every age and place? Or must you take someone else's word for their meaning?
3. **Feedback:** Are you rigorously trained to pick up cues about yourself from the reactions of others and from signals out of the environment? Do you have trouble accepting criticism and evaluating its worth? If you rely on test scores and teacher evaluations as stars to steer by you are in for a shock when you discover discrepancies between what you've been taught to think and reality.
4. **Analysis:** Can you take a new problem, break it into structural and procedural elements, gauge the relationships among those, reckon major outside influences, and do all this without expert help?
5. **Mirroring:** Have you learned to be everyone else as well as yourself? Can you be a chameleon at will? Or are you trapped in your own tight skin the way little people are. Can you fit into every group, even a group of your enemies, opting in and out as you please, yet remaining yourself?
6. **Expression:** Do you have a voice that's your own? Can you de-

liver that voice with clarity, style and force in writing and speaking? Without that, your ability to recruit allies will be feeble, and you will likely be swallowed up by someone whose expressiveness is superior to your own.

7. **Judgement:** Can you evaluate dispassionately? Can you see through falsehood? The society you are entering is a house of mirrors; little of what you see and few of those you meet will be what they appear. The most attractive personalities are invariably dishonest. How much chance did you have to develop judgement and test it?
8. **Adding Value:** Do you add value to every encounter, to every group of which you are a part? Do you even know what that means? If you aren't worth something to others, then truly you are worthless. That's Kurt Vonnegut speaking in one of his books, *Slaughterhouse Five,* I think.

There's more, but this is enough to start. You won't improve your grasp of these things by hanging around White River Junction and getting "A"s.

You are at present trapped in a labyrinth built by past generations; our entire nation, too; we're in a maze schooling can't help us to escape; the weakened nation you are inheriting is beyond school's power to strengthen. Let me show you why a little:

Social unrest is everywhere, a loss of faith in American leadership among our own citizenry and all over the world. Harvard and Dartmouth (as metaphors) have a lot to do with that loss of faith. It's been caused by a unilateral reorganization of work on the part of large employers who — I think it's fair to say — own our government. A reorganization planned at our elite universities where life is graceful and all problems knuckle under to method.

This coalition of social engineers exports American jobs to fatten the corporate bottom line, and imports foreign workers to accomplish the same end. Multi-billionaires like Bill Gates — who apparently isn't satisfied yet that he has enough money — are in the forefront of this movement. Then, there is a spreading practice called "contingent labor," where a company can save the cost of medical care, pensions, vacations, and the like by hiring on a temporary basis for the duration of a project. That has created a national proletariat with shallow roots in place of family, unable to plan any rational future because of job uncertainty and the need to be able to scramble wherever called just to subsist. Another big unilateral decision we have Harvard and Company to thank for is the idea of "Lean Production." Lean Production is more evidence that compassion is no longer a factor binding management to those who labor. In Lean Production the "Workforce" is stripped to the bone. As Frederick Taylor showed an earlier industrial establishment, it is then scientifically squeezed for every bit of juice it contains.

The unilateral reorganization of work is the reason for the growing gulf between rich and poor in America, the deepest such gulf on Planet Earth. It is destroying our historic middle class, destroying the working classes, and has broken the safety net around the poor — which depends on compassion, not efficiency, to maintain. The panic you feel growing around you will only stop by political action, not by better schooling.

The New Atlantis

College was transformed into a training ground for work right after WWII, work that is as corporations and government bureaus and university departments define work, not as real people do. A few colleges escaped this transformation, but none you are likely to have heard of and certainly not a single Ivy institution or similar.

The new collegiate landscape followed a formula set down by Francis Bacon in the 17th century in his utopian fragment, *The New Atlantis*, a book which while unknown to the circles you travel with has actually been held in the same high regard as religious scripture by important interests for centuries. In *The New Atlantis*, Bacon demonstrates how a world-university can act as a stabilizer for wealth and power. Externally.

This substitution of controlled utility as a justification for college replaced an earlier popular belief that it could be a place for reflection and pure intellectual development, rather like a monastic experience for the privileged young. College as utility fit a grander design, one of total and comprehensive social control, the dream of rulers since Solomon.

Under this new regimen which spread across the 19th century from a center in northern Germany, an intense degree of surveillance was put in place to make certain the common herd didn't stampede. Following the advice of two nineteenth century Italian social thinkers, Pareto and Mosca, the best talent of the underclasses was spotted early and drawn up into the command module to rob the masses of future leadership. Pragmatists like Pierce, James, Dewey, and Holmes, the new machiavellians, were responsible for this.

Society slowly became a laboratory in which big brother or his technological equivalent was always watching, and where punishment was always close at hand. To reach the goal of scientific management, a managed America had to be made rule-bound after the model of ancient Israel of Mishnah. But an impressive sophistication was obtained as well in the leadership of this project. If liberty was being curtailed in one area, license was encouraged in every zone of traditional morality. In sex, marriage, religion, family, the training of the young, an "anything goes" ethic was introduced and promoted steadily, a development which undercut any opposition from traditional moral centers by dividing children in school from their traditional sources of moral training at home.

I know how science-fictional this must all seem at 17 when personal realities are calling for attention in your life, but I have a staggering piece of symbolic evidence that what Bronx Science has taught you doesn't begin to describe the reality you'll be wrestling with in the years ahead.

School as Jail; Jail as School

The United States, traditional land of the free, now jails 25% of all prisoners on earth, 90% for non-violent crimes. With 5% of the global population, we are five times more eager than average to lock up our fellow citizens, six times more likely than China is to do the same thing.

How do you explain that, Kristina? Ask your friends and school counselors to explain it — they will look uncomfortable and avoid the question as if you made the figures up. If you want a definition for radical, here it is. Don't let it sit with you as a conversational oddity, it is a colossal fact, it means something stupendous to your future. Its ramifications are a good deal more significant for what your life will be than any college you choose to attend. It has happened for the same reason factory schooling happened.

Factory schooling replaced our historically libertarian forms of schooling at the beginning of the 20th century in order to standardize a kaleidoscopic pattern of individualized lives which tended to go off in many directions. A managerial utopia could not be made from such raw material; liberty plays no part in managerial efficiency — families like the MacAdams, the Gattos, and the Zimmers must be prevented from reproducing their eccentric outlooks or an essential subordination could never be achieved. This is why school had to be made compulsory, and why schools like Bronx Science were created — to minimize the influence that people like you and your ancestors would have on the whole.

Far from being a screwy pipe dream of your old granddad, or an ideologically driven phantasm of some cult, it is quite impossible to read heavily into history — even in its sanitized texts — without coming to something like the formulation I've just given you. For that reason alone, hard reading has been discouraged in the schools; if you read too much the official stories wear thin and blow away like smoke. All this garbage is right up on the surface to be seen unless attention can be diverted away by the irrelevant texts and procedures of schooling. Horace Mann himself called school "the best jail" to his financial backers, by which he meant that the jail you sentence your mind to when you go to school is harder to escape than any iron bars.

Thomas Jefferson was one of the few public figures who saw the dangers of a compulsory universal schooling scheme and was willing to chance it only if powerful safeguards could be erected to prevent the mental colonization it threatened. Those safeguards were only up a very short time before institutional schooling came along and broke them. Jefferson was familiar with Spinoza, the Dutch philosopher who designed systematic schooling expressly to put the minds and imaginations of the ordinary population to death. He knew that at best school would be about making clerks and servants, not thinkers and artists.

I spent ten years poking around the great school legend. What I learned is available to you without cost on my website, www.john taylorgatto.com where you'll find as my gift, 330,000 words on the underground history of American education to supplement those in this book. The connection between schooling as you know it, including collegiate schooling, and education is mostly a masterpiece of fabrication — on par with the medieval theory of four humors.

If you can force yourself to read Walter Lippman's early books, like *Phantom Public* and those of Sigmund Freud's nephew, Edward Bernays — the man who convinced ladies to take up smoking (and did public relations for Adolph Hitler), you'll be face to face with some of the ways this was done and the technicians who did it. Indeed, if you struggle hard to free yourself, Kristina, before you're dragged any further into the abyss by Dartmouth, I have evidence that personal miracles are still possible. I'm going to take a bit of that evidence from a surprising source.

The Great Imposters

The record of great imposters in recent years is one text you need to reflect upon for the priceless lesson it can teach about the supposedly vital training required to operate successfully inside certain occupations. Let's start with surgery and "Dr" Ferdinand Demara, a "Lieutenant Commander" on a Canadian warship operating off the Korean coast during the so-called Korean War.

Dr. Demara found himself facing an emergency appendectomy in the medical office of a small ship in heavy weather, a tough job for a real doctor (and he was far from that), calling on all the sea legs that a naval officer had developed at sea. But Demara was neither a sailor nor a medical man, only a cheeky imposter who had done stints as an airline pilot, a railroad engineer, and a Catholic priest in his interesting career.

And yet, laboring under these handicaps, he was able to successfully conclude the operation all alone (he didn't dare call for assistance), save a grateful man's life, and receive the highest honor the Canadian navy can bestow — an unfortunate conclusion to this wonderful story since the doctor Demara was pretending to be saw the press coverage and screamed.

The crime-and-punishment part of this story holds no interest for me so let me cut to the chase: All Demara needed to perform this tricky surgery was an illustrated textbook of how to perform the operation (which he found in the medical office library), some strong nerves (every imposter's stock in trade) and an ability to read, interpret photographs, and follow clear instructions. Anyone with those gifts can perform much surgery (not all, but much) by the numbers. Were we to unbundle much of the medical nonsense which guards the privileges of a dishonest profession, the standard of health around the world would soar — as it has in Cuba — while the princely incomes which make stock advisory services a fixture in the life of doctors would plummet.

At present, every serious medical condition on earth can be treated overseas in what amounts to luxury surroundings for about one-third the American cost; state-of-the-art dentistry is available in several places just across the US/Mexican border for a small fraction of American prices; and medicine of all sorts may be self-prescribed there for pennies on the dollar for what would bill at heart-breaking prices in the United States. Shouldn't our schoolchildren know these things in order to become "informed consumers"? But no school that taught them would remain open very long.

The Demara story sticks with me because something of the same sort happened to me in the 1980s in the year your mother graduated from MIT. We planned an expedition in her honor in the Mayan country: Palenque, Tikal, Copan, complete with volcanoes, fishing boats, orchid jungles, the works. But I ruined the trip by overplanning for contingencies; in a move to trick Fate I went down alone a month in advance hoping to drop off a wedding gift for your cousins Blake and Lauren who were being married on top of the volcano Popocatepetl (after climbing it first), and then take myself through the stages one after another to see they worked smoothly, and I wouldn't bumble around like a jerk when the real moments came.

That dress rehearsal cost me my right hip. Soaring past Monterrey on the way to Popo, and after that San Christobal, I ran into a gravel truck head on at 70 miles per hour. *Ay caramba!*

I woke on the operating table of a charity hospital in Monterrey with my right hip being bolted together with three huge pins. And promptly fainted. When I woke again I was in a ward with roaches swarming everywhere and a sleeping policeman by the bedside — I was under arrest for "damaging the highway." Next morning the doctor who operated, who wasn't a doctor at all but only a 23-year-old intern, was there when I awoke, with a big smile from ear to ear. He gave me a big hug and said with delight: "Everyone said you would die! I had never done this operation before. But I had a German textbook with pictures of every step to take and here you are — you are alive!"

So when I read about Demara I had good reason to know it was true. Here's another story to mull over: Suppose someone told you that with only a few hours classroom training that anyone would pilot a four engine airliner with some precision? I know, I know, it's crazy, isn't it? Yet there is a big hole in the ground where the World Trade Center used to be to put the doubters in their place.

And another hair-raising tale, well worth the Googling. A few years back the legendary financial house of Barings was brought down by an absolute rookie at the money game, Nick Leeson. Nick hoodwinked the savvy partners at Barings into believing he was making huge profits trading in and out of commodities, while in fact he was losing the company's shirt. In fact, he bankrupted the firm.

Leeson, the absolute amateur, was able to circumvent every safeguard a major financial house could ring around its assets.

The Barings story brings to mind the spectacular frauds perpetrated by the reckless brain trust at Enron, once America's seventh largest corporation and now defunct, and the rapid demise of Bear-Stearns, and Lehman Brothers, the fifth and fourth largest US investment banks, which succumbed to gambling with borrowed money — thirty times more borrowed money than it was worth, in Bear-Stearns' case.

Isn't it obvious, Kristina? Someone with nerve, ambition, well-developed observational skills, and some talent at mirroring can open the locked vaults at Barings, master medical procedures without the help of a medical school, fly airplanes, collapse tall buildings...and, if you remember Branson, build moon rockets without a high-school diploma, or like the elementary school dropout, Edison, light up the world.

Kara and Octavia, the Walkers

Look at your own potential with fresh eyes. The October 8, 2007 issue of *New Yorker* magazine featured a long account of a 37-year-old black artist named Kara Walker who had decided to take up art at the relatively old age of 24. The interview was conducted in a dimly lit bistro in Paris, France where Kara, surrounded by reporters, was being sketched by her nine-year-old daughter, Octavia. Octavia was so intent on her drawing that the article's writer commented on her ability to concentrate under the conditions.

As the story unfolded, we learned that little Octavia had serious aspirations to a career in fashion — and no interest at all in pats of the head or "A+"s. She was her mother's assistant in reality, in Paris to help with the exhibition, not as a cute thing to do. In one of Walker's short films at the museum, Octavia delivers the voice-over while a slave girl is being pursued by a white man. She chants, "I wish I were white," and "Maybe all this will dream away and I will disappear." Is that what you'd expect a nine-year-old to be doing, Kristina?

As I was reading the piece, the thin scrim of artificially extended childhood schools were invented to impose dropped away and I saw again, as I often do, the different world we could create if we dropped the pretense that childhood goes on very long past the age of seven.

The *New Yorker* article ended with Kara remembering an event that happened when Octavia was four — the same age as Branson when he walked about London. Octavia was watching her mother being interviewed by a swarm of reporters when suddenly, in agitation, she called out in a loud voice: "Kara Walker! Kara Walker! When is it going to be *my* turn?!" Age four, remember.

That's the point, Kristina. The school you're attending, Bronx Science, the college you hope to attend, Dartmouth, and indeed all schools in general exist to *delay* the ordinary — even the "bright" ordinary such as your Bronx Science classmates — from taking their turn. And the worst places seek to intimidate you into taking the turn *they* want you to take, *not the one your own spirit would have chosen.* It's an obscene form of mental colonization, a reckless waste of your all-too-short existence.

Most of those who are seduced into waiting their turn, by places like Bronx Science or Dartmouth, never actually get a turn, they grow old and die unrealized. Don't let that happen to you or the family ghosts will be very angry.

What Dartmouth and its brethren will do to you even more effectively than Bronx Science is to paralyze your ability to think for yourself, and do that enduringly enough that you'll risk losing your precious turn. I know how hard it is to wrap your mind around concepts like this at 17 when the thrill of your independent adult life is looming, filling your spirit with exciting prospects; and it's precisely *because* of your rightful need to be free at last that I write this way. It would fill me with sadness to see you escape one trap only to fall into another, deadlier one.

Let me give you some hard evidence that the people who built the schools and colleges you admire did not have *your* interests at heart, but their own. No single group was more influential in shaping our institutional school ladder than the pragmatic philosophers of Cambridge, Massachusetts. And no pragmatist carried more clout than Charles Pierce, the *eminence grise* behind William James and John Dewey. Listen to Pierce's mind at work in the 1870s as he contemplated the advent of forced schooling:

> Let the will of the state act, then, instead of that of the individual. *Let an institution be created* which shall have for its object to keep *correct doctrines* before the attention of the people, to reiterate them perpetually, and to teach them to the young, having at the same time *power to prevent contrary doctrines from being taught, advocated, or expressed.*
>
> Let all possible causes of a change of mind be removed from men's apprehension. *Let them be kept ignorant,* lest they should learn of some reason to think otherwise than they do. Let their passions be enlisted, so that they may regard... unusual opinions with hatred and horror. Then, let all men who reject the established belief be terrified into silence.... Let a list of opinions be drawn up to which no man of the least independence of thought can assent, and let the *faithful* be *required* to accept all these propositions in order to segregate them as radically as possible from the influence of the rest of the world [all emphases mine].

Kristina, this is the technology of modern management set down clearly for you to learn from. This is what John Dewey was after when he sold his patrons on the importance of reaching their ends through the means of schooling. And abandoning knowledge is a goal. This is the doctrine which drove William James in *Principles of Psychology* (1890), to assign habit-training, not intellectual development, the place of honor in schooling:

> Habit is the enormous fly-wheel of society, its most precious conservative agent. It alone is what...saves the children of fortune from the envious uprisings of the poor.... It alone prevents the hardest and most repulsive [jobs] from being deserted. It holds the miner in his darkness. It keeps different social strata from mixing.

For all your present scrappiness, Kristina, you are, like all of us, largely multiple layers of habits. Deliberately indoctrinated into you by agencies indifferent to your dignity, your personal sovereignty, and your welfare. It's up to you to hunt down relentlessly these "indwelling curiosity cut-offs" (as Kesey called them in *One Flew Over the Cuckoo's Nest*), and break their grip on your life. Then you will truly be free.

I want you to have a big, bold, free life, one lived with reckless courage, unquenchable compassion, and full reverence for the truth of things. The Dartmouths of the world are the enemies of truth. But whatever you decide, your Granny Janet and I will be with you in spirit and love. Good luck on the road ahead!

10

Incident at Highland High

Schooling and Education

Our time together is almost over. The book is nearly done. It's been a journal of the reflections of an old man whose thoughts, sometimes tormented, sometimes lucid, have been fixed on pedagogy, a term which has survived from Roman days to designate a special class of slave. Isn't that all you need to know? My mother said to me often when I was a little boy, "A word to the wise is sufficient." Pedagogy is the word. Under its influence I lived my life as a character in someone else's script. So I imagine did you. If my book can help you to escape, even partially, a similar destiny, I'll be content. The groaning it's cost to write will have been worth it.

What I reached for in these pages wasn't a diatribe although parts of them may seem so, nor was it only a critique although a critique is here, too. My ambition goes beyond having you merely accept my analysis; if I haven't provoked you into beginning an analysis of your own I'll be disappointed to have been, for just another time, only a schoolteacher. I need you to question your own schooling and the price you paid to sit for it; I need you to dig behind the illusions of education schooling produces; I need you to recognize how its imperial energy drives your understanding long after the classroom door seems to have closed forever.

School, which began as a sometimes thing in colonial America, no more than two hours a day a few months each year, isn't satisfied with the time set aside for it; today it resents even summer vacation in its drive to become a total institution: the familiar expression "lifelong learning" doesn't mean that at all, it means "lifelong schooling." More school is offered with a straight face by political leaders and corporate officials as the solution to growing social incoherence and other problems like aimlessness, incompetence, class hatred, and the rest of the dreary litany. But if less school helped cause these things, how can more school fix them?

School works against other roads to development besides itself. Family? A retrograde institution. Replace it. The synthetic families of utopian fiction must be superior because they were conceived by experts. Church? Off with its head! Can it be sensible to provide ordinary lives with the idea that any decision of experts can be appealed to a Higher Power? Tradition, ethnic loyalty, loyalty to place? Well, you know the drill. Off with their heads! And the damage school does to conceptions of individual sovereignty or ideals of liberty grows progressively more irreparable as each generation is robbed of its ability to parent the next.

There are several ways to measure the gulf between schooling and education. That step can't be avoided whichever method you chose. You can't draw a useful map to education if you don't know what the difference is. And like a good recipe it's less a matter of finding the perfect formula than understanding the right proportions of each ingredient to please yourself. The way you and I are schooled is identical for each of us: the way we get educated has little in common.

Sometimes schooling serves useful ends, too, but the minute it's ordered up centrally and imposed universally by the police power of the state, you need to start running from it (if your circumstances make that possible), or if they don't, you must cold-bloodedly plan to subvert it and sabotage it — all the while pretending with a smile on your face to cooperate. In that way you can inflict substantial damage on the institution which seeks to render you incomplete, without opening yourself to its punishments.

Kids helped to understand the mind-control aims of schooling can easily avoid its worst effects while gaining access to valuable raw material for observation and analysis. Someone who brings anthropological tools to elementary school — as Washington, Edison, and Carnegie did — can harvest rich understandings of their fellow citizens in embryo, and of the adults hired to hold them captive — men and women under no less duress than the herd they oversee.

In hunting for the difference between school and education, consider these layers: Schooling is organized by command and control from without; education is self-organized from within; school disconnects its clientele from other primary sources of learning. It must do that to achieve administrative efficiency; education sets out to provide a set of bountiful connections which are random, willful, promiscuous, even disharmonious with one another — understanding that the learning of resourcefulness, self-sufficiency, and invention will inevitably involve surprising blends of things, things impossible to predict or anticipate in advance.

In education the student is awakened to the critical role natural feedback loops play in becoming independent. Feedback loops attended to closely — not circumscribed by rules — create customized circuits of self-correction rather than a slavish need to follow the generalized direction of others. But schooling is bound on the other hand to emphasize rules made by others. It's impossible even to imagine a school that could allow free will deviation from its programmes, except to the most trivial degree.

Education is never committed to subject knowledge, it always tends to regard things in rich contexts. Subject-learning is what schools do because their intention is to create clerks, and specialists, who themselves are merely a fancy form of clerk. But over and over again in the sciences and elsewhere we've come to understand that cross-fertilization, mixing the academic disciplines (and more) is the powerful driver of scientific advance. John Kanzius, a name referred to in an earlier chapter, was able to invent a new tool against cancerous tumors precisely because he wasn't a specialist in cancer research, or even a college graduate.

~

The components of education are so diverse they establish a permanent internal state of dialectical argument. Certainty is never achieved in the educated mind; creative destruction — the potent energy of capitalism according to Schumpeter — is always at work in the educated spirit, it seeks to find holes in orthodox theory, it works constantly to create replacements for what "everyone knows to be true."

On the other hand, memory — not synthesis or argument — is the dominant element in schooling. Because of that impediment, "A" students are robbed test by test of their ability to think for themselves and to listen to the cues of their feedback circuits.

Year after year, the International Happiness Survey reports only three conditions necessary to judge your own life a happy one: 1) good relationships 2) good health 3) satisfying work. But school, as I showed you earlier, sets up conditions in which bad health is difficult to escape, relationships are given no time or space to grow in (and segregation of similar backgrounds in so-called tracking schemes makes it nearly certain that class prejudice will flourish (putting the possibility of relationships with those different from oneself out of reach for students so tracked.). And the work imposed in schooling virtually never is directed to answering the compelling questions of youth.

The Dark World

But have I made too much of this? Can the use of combative metaphors like "weapons" and "the dark world" be anything more than language drawn from adolescent fantasy, the cut worm's resentment of the plow? School has failings, yes, but surely it's an essential institution, and aren't all its deficiencies amenable to rational correction, yet none to name calling?

Have I made too much of the past, for instance? Have I been too hard on the coalition of eugenicists, utopians, business leaders, churchmen, Darwinists, racists, and high academics who planted the institution in North America in the last part of the nineteenth century? They meant no harm, just the reverse, and in any case they are all dead now. Shouldn't the present moment be devoted to problem-solving? Can't past shortcomings be ascribed to ordinary ineptitude, venality, imperfect leadership and such like?

You must decide these questions for yourself, but as for me, I concluded long ago that some deliberate intent was (and is) at work on the school institution, that it operates far from public access, and until it is confronted the term "school reform" is meaningless. Unless the ends of the operation are put on public trial, and its sexual relationships with economics and social management exposed to the light and ended, each reform effort will only be another illusion, another room added to the national house of mirrors.

But you'll have to convince yourself of the substance of my allegation, that some sort of dark matter, some powerful but invisible force is at work in schooling. If you are to become strong enough to defend yourself, and your family I can't do the work for you, you can't memorize my conclusions. To that end I'm going to tell you three hair-raising school stories which will seem, at first, inexplicable to you, aberrations perhaps. Your job will be to interpret what they mean, if anything. As you hear these stories, try to imagine which officials, located where, could finally have signed-off on these initiatives. And in whose interests. As you think about them, keep in mind that no sane bureaucrat, no matter how highly placed, would dream of initiating anything which might embarrass or anger the managers of things. Keep Hobbes in mind as you reflect, power is never where it seems to be.

For myself, I tried to find a simple explanation to put these stories into the normal course of things, but try as I might they wouldn't fit. Only a darkness at work, reachable not by common experience but through historical, sociological, psychological, theological, political and philosophical research, could reveal the causes, it seemed to me. Hence this book.

But you may disagree. Perhaps as Alexander saw a simple solution to the Gordian knot and Occam saw that in science simple explanations cut closer to the truth, you'll see an explanation I missed.

Meanwhile, three stories: one from Nuremberg, Germany in 2008; one from Highland, New York, in 2004, and one from Walden, Vermont in 1991. I could tell you many more in a similar vein which suggest to me a dark force living inside the house of mirrors we call school; but if these three don't waken your suspicions, then the rest wouldn't either.

Incident at Nuremberg

On January 29, 2008, a sixteen-year-old girl, Melissa Busekros, living in Nuremberg, Germany, was forcibly removed from her home by fifteen policemen and assorted city officials and placed under psychiatric investigation. Her crime: homeschooling. When I heard of the incident, I wrote the German ambassador in Washington to register my disgust:

Dear Mr. Ambassador:

Homeschooling in Germany was legal until 1937 when it was suddenly banned by the Nazi government. I'm writing to enquire why Hitler's ban is still being enforced 72 years later? In whose interests is this proscription kept? For what specific purposes? You will be aware, I know, that between 2½ and 3 million Americans are currently being homeschooled. One of them, travelling through Germany, recently informed me of the Melissa Busekros affair and asked my help in understanding the matter. Hence this letter.

Your court ordered social work authorities to apprehend Melissa in forceful language which I shall quote: "The Jugendamt is hereby instructed and authorized to bring the child — if necessary by force — to a hearing. Police support may be obtained for this purpose."

A number of details bother me about this court order. In the first place nothing in Melissa's history would suggest that police intervention was necessary. A simple letter commanding the attendance of the family at a hearing would have been obeyed. Then, she was interrogated for 240 minutes at a psychiatric clinic about her reasons for homeschooling when the movement had been international for about four decades (in its modern renaissance) and had produced many distinguished men and women over that time — including the head of the Human Genome Project.

The findings of this interrogation were that Melissa was suffering from a mysterious, fast-growing disease called " school phobia," a medical condition which, the official report continued, had resulted in her development being "delayed by one year."

Is it to be understood that Germany believes such a finely calibrated yardstick exists and yet the rest of the world is unaware of it? On the basis of this flimsy bit of pseudo-science an emergency was adjudged to exist — one so serious Melissa's contact with her own family had to be immediately terminated? This is crazy on the face of it. What reasoning, what philosophy, what values hide behind this action?

Two days after interrogation, fifteen police descended upon the Busekros home accompanied by the judge in the case and the State Youth Staff assigned to Melissa's emergency. Would it be cynical to assume that a generous contingent of media reporters came along to commemorate the event?

By an official statement of the German court the arresting authorities were absolved of responsibility. The court said: "The cause of this forced escort was set in place by the parents' illegal conduct. The education administration will not recognize so-called homeschooling and will act in proportionate measure." Proportionate? Fifteen police?

The official report also states that the German education authority will act "to bring convictions of the family into line." What tools will be employed to discipline convictions, Mr. Ambassador? That sounds rather ominous, sir. Long ago during the centuries of witchcraft frenzy in which the Germans killed more women than all the rest of the nations of Europe combined, the tools included rack, thumbscrews, pressing with weights, amputation of body parts, fire, etc. Then later, between 1933 and 1945, the palette of instruments was enlarged to include concentration camps, quicklime, freezing, and other technically advanced methods carefully described in the minutes of "The Doctors' Trial" in postwar Nuremberg. And what of today, Mr. Ambassador?

My mother's side of the family descends from Germany, so it's partially as a man whose DNA is German-derived that I feel alarmed the German madness is beginning again, symbolized by the terror inflicted on a sixteen-year-old girl. Some famous Germans have attributed your nation's sickening record to attitudes enshrined in your treatment of the young. Erich Remarque, author of *All Quiet on the Western Front,* tracked the causes of WWI directly to German schoolmasters and their lies, and Dietrich Bonhoeffer, the famous Protestant theologian executed by Hitler, pronounced WWII the "inevitable" product of German schooling. German war-lovers like Martin Luther, Frederick the Great, Otto von Bismarck, and Adolf Hitler, are, I think, red herrings — transient phenomena which mask what actually has taken place in your part of the world since the Old Norse Religion: an obsession with system, a search for The Master Formula. In systems logic, concepts like liberty and individual rights are direct attacks on the integrity of systems. Fichte saw that no efficient national management was possible as long as the ordinary population regarded itself as sovereign individuals possessing free will and imagination; therefore he demanded compulsory schooling aimed at removing these things.

In the short run this form of mind control works to convert your ordinary population into a very manageable mass. It certainly has given the Germans the reputation they enjoy worldwide as dependable automatons. But in the long run it cripples your economic prospects. Think only of the recent debacle with ThyssenKrupp dumping its Phoenix Steel plant on "gullible" China. Chinese peasants moved the plant in one-third the time German engineers estimated and Phoenix has been a money-maker for China ever since, while rule-bound Krupp through its bad judgement has taken employment away from 10,000 German breadwinners.

And the final irony, of course, was that the man in charge of taking Phoenix away was mostly homeschooled, a common reality in rural China for millennia.

~

I got no answer to my letter. As a bureaucrat, what could he say?

Incident at Highland High

On March 5, 2004, I drove to Highland High School in prosperous Rockland County north of New York City at the invitation of a school board member, John Jankiewicz. Mr. J. was a total stranger until he made the offer to speak, but his letter of enquiry intrigued me. He was concerned that the Germanicized schooling at Highland, built around the principles of behavioral psychology as almost all American schooling is, was hurting future prospects for Highland graduates. It bothered him. John was himself an impressively educated man with creative talent as a hydraulic engineer which earned him a global reputation for the projects he had designed around the world.

I looked forward to meeting him, but not to speaking before juniors and seniors at a rich exurban high school, because I knew from past experience how hard it is to talk to self-satisfied teenagers. When I got to the school early to size up the place, my suspicions were confirmed. Its parking lot was filled with high-end student vehicles and the general demeanor among the kids I saw was one of self-satisfaction. It reminded me of the Crystal Springs Upland School, a wealthy private school in coastal California whose claim to notoriety was its former student, Patty Hearst. When I went there to speak, I heard a student say that the faculty cars were so low-class that even his gardener drove a better one.

But at both places students paid a very high price for enrollment in the club; their arrogance masked a mediocre command of intellectual skills and they were being steeped like tea bags in a climate of non-stop dishonesty about college preparation, about the decisive effect that grade averages and standardized tests scores would supposedly have on their future.

The unspeakable prospect of not being accepted at a prestige college or even not being accepted at all was the ground upon which academic studies were constructed. The great question for a young woman or man was surviving the scrutiny of those invisible judges who held the scales of human worth. That was of central interest. That life had recently been demonstrated to be possible in fantastic variety in the total absence of light and photosynthesis, by a mixture of chemicals and heat alone, might have been of interest to a geek, but it had nothing to offer the future managers of geeks.

Among the many secrets withheld from the students at Highland (or Crystal Springs) was the fact that colleges were businesses before they were anything else, businesses desperate for warm bodies in order to meet payrolls. They had little to worry about in finding a place which would gladly exchange its degree for a bag of money, and while elite college admission couldn't be guaranteed because the number of applicants always exceeded the number of seats, "C" students like Al Gore, John Kennedy, John Kerry, George Bush, John McCain (who finished 895th out of 900 graduates at Annapolis, and lost five airplanes of which he was a pilot) and Franklin Roosevelt had no difficulty being admitted to elite colleges and graduating from them.

Since I knew the kids at Highland would be worried about college, I decided to build my talk around the actual situation and criteria for admission — not around the fantasy schooling uses to maintain discipline. I would aim to undermine the foundation of their vague fears — which the school like most schools had exploited to the maximum. The strategy wasn't to preach, but instead to direct attention to the masses of prominent people, past and present, who had somehow managed to sidestep the big school lie and to make success without it. For instance, you already know the computer industry was built on the vision of dropouts; you know how each of our Nobel Prize creative writers was a dropout; you know that the entertainment industry in all its facets is overwhelmingly dominated by dropouts, the fast food industry, too; and how the politicians we entrust national policy to were almost uniformly mediocre students.

I was armed with information from *The New York Times* which put the standardized test scores of superintendents, principals, and teachers at almost the very bottom of twenty major occupational groups in that regard, and with superintendents being the worst of the worst! I told the kids (quietly, I swear) to have their parents demand that every school employee in their district be required to post their own grade/test records prominently on their doors and that this would cause the whole sorry house of mirrors to shatter like Humpty Dumpty.

Once these seeds were planted, all subject to easy verification, they would grow on their own; in these minds closed tightly as clams by prosperity and the climate of fear I believed Highland was retailing as a crowd control device, this mass of anomalous data would act as a strong acid burning minds open.

The most effective single body of information I transmitted was about the admission policies at Harvard, Stanford, Yale, Princeton, and similar prestigious places, places, which reject huge numbers of valedictorians, perfect GPA averagers, and perfect SAT scores every year in favor of applicants with "a record of distinction" (as Harvard admissions director Marlyn McGrath was quoted as saying a few years ago). Have you started a successful business? Have you founded a charity? Have you sailed around the world alone, walked from Tierra del Fuego to Point Barrow, Alaska without professional help; can you take a tractor down to its component parts and reassemble it all by yourself...?

Can teenagers do these things? Of course they can. High school dropout Richard Branson, who you heard about in "Walkabout: London," is shown in my daily newspaper this morning (July 29, 2008) cracking a bottle of champagne over the nose of the spaceship he just completed to carry tourists into space at some $200,000 a seat (more than 250 have paid so far). It's named *Eve* in honor of his single mother, Eve Branson, who had the foresight to encourage him to walk miles on his own through London at the age of four. Although only a small fraction of the total, a much larger absolute number of teenagers is already well launched into real life than you can possibly imagine if you've swallowed the school myth hook, line and sinker.

The student response was electrifying. Rather than the indifference to a more generalized message that I had encountered at Crystal

Springs, the student audience was rapt, completely attentive, as if somehow able to perceive how important it was to cast off the assumptions which held them in thrall.

At this point I need you to visualize the style of this talk, for reasons which will be clear in a little while. At no point in my delivery was I excitable, histrionic, condemnatory, or anything other than perfectly calm and even-voiced. Each fact I laid out was referenced from some mainstream information source capable of being checked for verification.

And then it happened.

Suddenly a police detail threw the doors of the auditorium open with a loud noise and invaded the room! The officer in charge shouted through a bullhorn, "This assembly is over! Leave the auditorium at once! Return to class! Remain calm! Follow your teachers! Leave the room at once!"

It was easily the strangest moment of my life. Nobody in the room *wasn't* calm, except the police!

The officer in charge shouted through a bullhorn: "This assembly is over! Leave the auditorium at once!" and saying that, he walked double-time to where I stood at the front of the auditorium, fixed my eye the way a red-tailed hawk regards a sparrow. He snapped, "Leave the room at once. This lecture is over!" I had no doubt I would be arrested if I failed to comply.

Had the school received a bomb threat? No. I was the bomb. As I left the building, Jankiewicz caught up with me to report that McCarthy, the superintendent, found my talk so inflammatory he called the police to stop it. Think about that. My voice had never raised above a conversational tone. I used no bad language. I hadn't mooned the audience or exposed myself. It's true that Highland didn't require the degree of overkill Nuremberg used to shut Melissa Busekros down, there were only three cops sent to shut me up, but the principle — I hope you can see — was no different.

Nor was this the end. I had been scheduled to speak to parents that evening at the school. McCarthy cancelled that talk, too, refusing to allow the school to be used as a venue. The room had been paid for, the students would have been long gone, only adults would be in attendance, but none of that made a difference. No one in Highland, New York, was to be allowed to hear facts which you've read in this book.

Three days afterward, on April 7, 2004, *The Mid-Hudson Highland Post*, a newspaper out of Poughkeepsie just across the Hudson from Highland, reported the story — at least part of it. The news account was titled: "Rendered Speechless — Advocate for Reform Brings Controversy."

Not a word about the police incursion was in the story, but apart from that it added several illuminating details I would otherwise not have known. Superintendent McCarthy was identified as the individual who had stopped the lecture, for instance. But the dispatch of a unit that size for a small town must have been no small matter. It seemed to demand an answer to why the building principal (who must have reported the "emergency" I represented by telephone to the district office) hadn't simply come discreetly to the microphone and told me to wrap things up quickly, perhaps saying "something has come up." Or why, if he lacked the presence of mind to do that, the superintendent hadn't requested he do so before recourse to the police was considered? And finally, why the Highland police dispatcher hadn't sent one officer, rather than three? Was the assumption that anyone so crazed as to bring objective data to high school students must be on drugs, and would pose a danger if a show of force wasn't made?

The newspaper story contained the superintendent's justification for his action as my screening a violent film for student consumption. Since the film in question had been shown nationally on PBS and on the Discovery Channel, it hardly seems likely this was the actual motive, and what gave the lie away more than anything to the superintendent's explanation was the cancellation of the evening parents meeting. One teacher was quoted by the reporter as saying her classes had exciting discussions following the talk. They were "eager to discuss the issues raised," she said, "Unfortunately our school didn't allow that to happen."

The last chapter in this weird tale is as creepy to me as the incident itself. On May 15, 2007, when I realized that my experience at Highland was going to be a part of this book, I sent individual letters to the superintendent, the school principal, the parents association, and the student newspaper. I asked each to give their own version of the story, and promised to print them unedited. This was over a year ago as I write this — not a phone call, a postcard, or other response has reached me — exactly the same silent treatment I got from the German ambassador.

Nada, de nada, y nada, pues nada ... Highland is a clean, well lighted place, but a bad representative of America's best traditions. Or so it seems to me:

> ...we set ourselves the task of inoculating youth...at an age when human beings are still unspoiled.
>
> — Adolf Hitler. 1 May, 1937

Because you choose not to see the dark world school represents, because you only pay attention to its stupidities, it gets worse all the time.

Do I mean to imply that Highland High School is the worst school in America? Hardly. For all I know it's one of the best; certainly it's one of the richest. What you need to ask yourself is how many school districts from coast to coast find truth unbearable because it gets in the way of their real mission. The growing incoherence of American society stands upon a foundation of forced schooling in fancy places like Highland, no less than in Harlem, Watts, or East St. Louis.

Incident at Walden

Until 1991 Walden, Vermont — a picture-perfect village in a picture-book state, the most rural state in America — had four beautiful one-room schoolhouses, each different, each set apart from the others, each with a genuine swimming hole made by damming a creek the way country people have done since the beginning of time. The reading and math scores from these schools were substantially above the state average, the children so happy and healthy-looking that when I visited I secretly teared up at one point when confronted with the stark comparison between them and the kids I was familiar with in Manhattan. It goes without saying that the parents whose children were associated with such charming places were delighted, and anxious to help out in any way they could.

Since I'm about to cast the idyllic state of Vermont as a villain in this third unbelievable story, I need to tell you first that every encounter I've ever had with this state — before I came to Walden — was an absolute joy. Let me illustrate with my favorite state capitol experience ever, and I've visited them all. One day in 1990, I was called to speak in Montpelier, Vermont, at the college, while I was still New York Teacher of the Year. Arriving in that grand little city a day early, I decided to walk to the capitol building and poke around to kill some time. The atmosphere inside the handsome structure was so laid-back and low-key, I decided to go to the governor's office and leave a note of thanks for him with the secretary, thanks to his stewardship of this uniquely personalized state.

The door was open so I walked in. No secretary was around. I waited five minutes and still no secretary, so I knocked gingerly on the governor's door, once, twice, and then the door opened. Peering in I could clearly see — no governor. Since there was no guard in the corridor outside either to ask permission of, I decided to leave a note in the middle of the governor's desk and leave, but when I leaned over to do that some impish Pittsburgh Scotch-Irish spirit whispered in my ear, "Why not sit in his chair behind his desk and see what it feels like to be governor of Vermont?"

And so I did.

A minute or two passed before my better half asked me what I would say if the governor walked in? Would I tell him that I'd be with him in a minute? And with that discomfiting thought I got up and left. I tell you this because I doubt if that could happen in any other place in America (perhaps Montana?) and in any case, not many.

In April of 1991, as I remember, I was asked to come to Walden to speak in defense of the one-room schools which were threatened with destruction by the state on the grounds that making them wheelchair friendly and installing handicap railings, etc. — as required by Federal law — was too expensive to justify. A concrete block "regional" school was to be built in their place and kids bused to it from up to fifty miles away. Everyone associated with the schools was in shock. This measure had been voted down several times in past years, but this time the state was baring its teeth. If the proposal was voted down again, the state would cut off funds to the town for school aid, and use its right of eminent domain to tear them down anyway.

As soon as I got to the home of the family hosting me, I asked to see the government proposal. You wouldn't have needed to be a lawyer or an accountant to see that the estimates for construction on the four schools were wildly out of line — a quarter million dollars, I recall, when 25 thousand would have been overkill. Fortunately (or so I thought) I knew a famous architect who taught at the University of Vermont, and I told my hosts I would ask him to testify against the accuracy of the state estimate. And so I called. Some hours later he was with us, reading the relevant papers. "These estimates are ten times higher than actual costs would be," he said emphatically. He told us it was a common trick employed by local governments when a decision had already been made, contracts already quietly pledged — he knew the firm which had been given assurances it would be building the replacement school. But he declined to testify.

"Why not, for pity's sake?" I asked him.

"If I did, I'd never get another job in the state of Vermont, that's why," he answered.

I spoke as eloquently as I knew how at the church that evening, where every resident in the town was in attendance. But the state's repeated threats had caused a tide of fear to suppress any further resistance. The tiny town passed the bond issue the state had demanded, went deeply into debt, and built the major eyesore in eastern Vermont, a big, boxy, mostly windowless factory school that had been forced upon it.

Once again, you will have to decide whether the dark world I perceive, where school decisions are made which defy common sense, rationality, and even familiar greed, are real or only phantoms in a disgruntled schoolteacher's imagination. If you decide I have a piece of the truth, you must help me sabotage this thing because, like Bear Stearns, Fannie Mae, and so much else in the new world order which has been built in America, our government thinks some companies are too big to be allowed to fail, and that schooling is too important to allow education to get in its way.

Afterword

> But whoever causes one of these little ones to stumble, it would be better for him if a millstone were hung around his neck, and he were thrown into the sea.
>
> — Mark 9:42

Invitation to an Open Conspiracy: The Bartleby Project[1]

If you read this to the end, you'll discover that I'm inviting you to join a real conspiracy, call it an open conspiracy, with real consequences on millions of real lives. I know that sounds megalomaniacal, but be patient. If we pull this off, a great many will bless us, although the school industry few will curse us. This is about a project to destroy the standardized testing industry, one in which you, personally, will be an independent unit commander. This adventure is called "The Bartleby Project," for reasons you'll learn in just a little while. And keep in mind as you read, this has nothing to do with test reform. It's about test *destruction.*

We've all taken these tests. After graduation few of us think back on this ugly phenomenon unless we have little ones of our own being

[1] © 2008 by John Taylor Gatto. This piece may be circulated without cost on the Internet, but only if used uncut and cost-free. The Bartleby Project is taken from Mr. Gatto's book, *Weapons of Mass Instruction,* New Society Publishers 2008.

tested, and have to live through the agony of watching them stumble. We lose touch with the rituals of testing because, upon entering adult life, we inevitably discover that the information these glorified jigsaw puzzles generates is unreliable, and very misleading — absolutely nobody ever asks after the data. We see that those who test well are more often circus dogs than leaders of the future.

Nothing inside the little red schoolhouse does more personal and social damage than the numbers and rank order these tests hang around the necks of the young. Although the scores correlate with absolutely nothing of real value, the harm they cause is real enough: such assessments are a crowning glory of the social engineers who seized final control of institutional schooling during the presidency of Franklin Roosevelt. They constitute a matchless weapon of social control, wreaking havoc on winners and losers alike. Standardized testing is the tail wagging the entire monster of forced institutional schooling.

The frequent ceremonies of useless testing — preparation, administration, recovery — convert forced schooling into a travesty of what education should be; they drain hundreds of millions of days yearly from what might otherwise be productive pursuits; they divert tens of billions of cash resources into private pockets. The net effect of standardized testing is to reduce our national wealth in future generations, by suffocating imagination and intellect, while enhancing wealth for a few in the present. This occurs as a byproduct of "scientifically" ranking the tested so they can be, supposedly, classified efficiently as human resources. I hope the chapters of this book have done some damage to these assumptions, enough to recruit you as a leader in The Bartleby Project. If you show the way, others will follow.

We've reached a point in North America where it isn't enough to claim moral loftiness by merely denouncing them or muttering about them in books and essays which only true believers read. Standardized testing, which has always been about standardization and never about quality standards, must no longer be debated, but brutally and finally destroyed if schooling is ever again to take up a mission of intellect and character enhancement. And so, as I told you earlier, you'll be invited to lead — not join, but lead — a plan to cut the testing empire off at the knees; a plan to rip its heart out swiftly and cheaply. An incidental byproduct of the Bartleby Project will be to turn the men and women who create and supervise these murderous exercises into pariahs, but that isn't the point.[2]

No organization will be required to oversee this simple plan — or, rather, thousands of organizations will be; all local, all uncoordinated. Otherwise, we will be certain to be co-opted, marginalized, corrupted — as all reform organizations become in time: and one as powerful as the Bartleby concept would be quickly subjected to sabotage were it centralized. To make this work — and soon you'll know what it looks like specifically — requires exactly the kind of courage it took to sledgehammer the first chunks out of the Berlin Wall, a currency in ready abundance among teenagers — the rightful leaders.

I'll briefly mount a case why such a project is needed and then introduce you to its spiritual godfather, Bartleby the Scrivener.

On May 8, 2008, the *New York Sun* reported that despite legal mandates which require physical education be offered every school day, only one kid out of every twenty-five received even the legal minimum of 24 minutes a day. The New York City comptroller was quoted by the *Sun*, saying that physical training was a major concern of parents. But then, parents have had no significant voice in school for over a century. The story gets even darker than you realize.

[2] Many test creators are fully aware of radical shortcomings in the tests they devise, and aware as well of severe political misuse of their assessment creations. Still, they continue to serve the testing regime for the personal benefits gained. For a recent example of this, see test expert Daniel Koretz's book, *Measuring Up* (Harvard University Press, 2008), in which the damage tests cause is someone else's responsibility, not Dr. Koretz's; to be deplored, of course between paychecks. Should these people be held responsible for long-term consequences of their work — "generating a feeling of inferiority...that may affect their hearts and minds in a way unlikely ever to be undone," to borrow Justice Warren's language from the Brown case?

Quietly, over the past decade, a national epidemic of obesity and diabetes has appeared in children as young as five. The connections between food, lack of exercise, and these twin plagues have been recognized for a long time. Diabetes is the principal cause of blindness and amputations in the US, and obesity is the leading cause of heart disease and self-loathing. That the non-fat are revolted by the fat, and discriminate heavily against them should not be a mystery, even to the stupid. Fat kids are punished cruelly in classrooms and on the playground.

In the face of these sobering facts, that thousands of schools still serve familiar fast food — and also non-proprietary fatty foods like liverwurst and bologna as nutrition — should have already caused you to realize that school is literally a risk to the mental and physical health of the young. Coupled with the curious legal tradition which makes serious lawsuits against school-generated human damage impossible, I hope you will try to convince yourself that behind the daily noise and squalor, a game is afoot in this institution which has little to do with popular myth. Standardizing minds is a big part of that game.

In the news story cited, a representative of New York City's Board of Education declares, "We're beginning to realize student health is a real core subject area." Think about that. The city has had a hundred-year near-monopoly over children's daily lives and it's only *beginning* to realize that health is important? Where is evidence of that realization? Don't all schools still demand physical confinement in chairs as a necessary concomitant of learning?[3]

[3] The issue of school immobility is more complicated than physical health alone. As a former college admissions researcher, Mitchell Stevens, writes in *Creating a Class: College Admissions and the Education of Elites* (Harvard University Press, 2007), at elite colleges "the physical appearance of human bodies" matters as much as grades. Bodies are visible embodiments of social class, he tells us. Desirable applicants look good, in plain language. Physically impressive applicants are strongly preferred — although the group made soft and doughy by twelve years spent fixed in seats and eating a diet rich in fats are not let into the secret by official schooling. Ignoring this powerful reality which blankets every corner of after-graduation reality is a most punishing weapon.

When lack of exercise has clearly been fingered as a main road to diabetes and obesity, and both conditions are well-understood to lead to blindness, amputations, heart disease, and self-hatred, how can law only provide 24 minutes of exercise a day, and be so poorly enforced that only one in twenty-five gets even that? Doesn't that tell you something essential about the managers of schooling? At the very least, that 96 percent of all schools in New York City break the law with impunity in a matter threatening the health of students. What makes it even more ominous is that school officials are known far and wide for lacking independent judgment and courage in the face of bureaucratic superiors; but something in this particular matter must give them confidence that they won't be held personally liable.

You must face the fact that an outlaw ethic runs throughout institutional schooling. It's well-hidden inside ugly buildings, masked by dull people, mindless drills, and the boring nature of almost everything associated with schools, but make no mistake — under orders from somewhere, this institution is perfectly capable of lying about life-and-death matters, so how much more readily about standardized testing?

If the bizarre agenda of official schooling allows its representatives to tell the press that after a hundred years they're *beginning* to learn what Plato and Aristotle wrote eloquently about thousands of years ago, and that privileged sanctuaries like Eton, Harrow, Groton, and St. Pauls have practiced since their inception, that physical health depends upon movement, you should be reluctant to assign credibility to *any* school declaration. Under the right pressure from somewhere, schools can easily be brought to act against the best interests of students or faculty.

This is what has happened with standardized testing, post-WWII. Some teachers know, and most all teachers feel in their bones, that the testing rituals cause damage. But human nature being what it is, only a few dare resist, and these are always eventually discovered and punished.

I began my own schooling in 1940 in the gritty industrial section of Pittsburgh ironically named "Swiss-vale," continued it for the most part in the equally gritty industrial exurb, Monongahela, during WWII and its aftermath, and concluded my time, served forcibly, in the green hills of western Pennsylvania, very near where Colonel Washington's late-night killing of French officer Jumonville precipitated the French and Indian War (Washington didn't do the killing himself, but he took the heat).

As compensation for confinement, schools in those days were generally places of visible morality, powerfully egalitarian, and often strongly intellectual under the rough manners of the classroom. Faculties were always local, which meant among other things that each school employee had a local reputation as a neighbor and citizen; they existed as people as well as abstract functions. Curriculum prepared far away, and standardized testing, was hardly in evidence even at the end of the school sequence for me, in the 1950s. Each classroom at my high school, Uniontown High, was personalized to a degree which would be considered dangerously eccentric today, and hardly tolerable.

And yet, boys and girls schooled that way had just finished ruining the tightly schooled dictatorships of the planet. We boasted often to ourselves, teenagers of the 1940s and 1950s, that unlike those unfortunate enough to live outside the US, *we* carried no identification papers, feared no secret police. Compared to the exotic liberty of those days of my boyhood, American society of sixty years later smacks a bit too much of a police state for comfort. To imagine old ladies being patted down for explosives at airports, or the IRS invasion of one's home, or the constant test rankings and dossiers of behavior managed through schooling; to imagine machinery purchased for home use spying on intimate choices and reporting those choices to strangers, would have been inconceivable in 1950.

A river of prosperity was lifting all boats in the US as I finished my own public schooling in 1953. My father was a cookie salesman for Nabisco, a man with no inheritance or trust fund, yet he could cover my tuition at Cornell, own a new car, send my sister to college, pay for clarinet lessons for me and painting lessons for my sister, and put something aside for retirement. Schooling was considered important in those days, but never as *very* important. Too many unschooled people like my father and mother carried important responsibilities too well for pedagogical propaganda to end the reign of America's egalitarian ethic.

The downward spiral in school quality began in the 1950s with changes which went unnoticed. Schools were "rationalized" after the German fashion; increment by increment they were standardized from coast to coast. By 1963, standardized tests were a fixture, although very few extended them any credibility; they were thought of as a curious break from classroom routine, a break imposed for what reason nobody knew, or cared. Even in the 1950s, curriculum was being dumbed down, though not to the levels reached in later years. Teachers were increasingly carpet-baggers, from somewhere outside the community in which they taught. Once it had actually been a legal requirement to live within the political boundaries of the school district, just as it was for police, fire fighters, and other civil servants, but gradually families came to be seen as potential enemies of the "professional" staff; better to live far enough away so they could be kept at arm's length.

Morality in schools was replaced with cold-blooded pragmatism. As Graham Greene has his police chief say, in *Our Man in Havana*, "We only torture people who expect to be tortured." Ghetto kids were flunked and nearly flunked because that was their expectation; middle-class/upper-middle-class kids were given Cs, Bs and even As, because they and their parents wouldn't tolerate anything else.

School order came to depend upon maintaining good relations with the toughest bullies, covertly affirming their right to prey upon whiners and cry-babies (though never cry-babies from politically potent families). The intellectual dimension was removed from almost all classrooms as a matter of unwritten policy, and since test scores are independent of intellect, those teachers who tried to hold onto mental development as a goal, rather than rote memorization, actually penalized their students and themselves where test scores were the standard of accomplishment.

Horace Mann's ideal of common schooling was put to death after WWII; students were sharply divided from one another in rigid class divisions justified by standardized testing. Separation into winners and losers became the ruling dynamic.

By 1973, schools were big business. In small towns and cities across the land schoolteaching was now a lucrative occupation — with short hours, long vacations, paid medical care, and safe pensions; administrators earned the equivalent of local doctors, lawyers, and judges.

Eccentricity in classrooms was steeply on the wane, persecuted wherever it survived. Tracking was the order of the day, students being steered into narrower and narrower classifications supposedly based on standardized test scores. Plentiful exceptions existed, however, in the highest classifications of "gifted and talented," to accommodate the children of parents who might otherwise have disrupted the smooth operation of the bureaucracy.

But even in these top classifications, the curriculum was profoundly diminished from standards of the past. What was asked of prosperous children in the 1970s would have been standard for children of coal miners and steel workers in the 1940s and 1950s. Many theories abound for why this was so, but only one rings true to me: From WWII onwards it is extremely easy to trace the spread of a general belief in the upper realms of management and academy that most of the population was incurably feeble-minded, permanently stuck at a mental level of twelve or under. Since efforts to change this were doomed to be futile, why undergo the expense of trying? Or to put a humane cast on the argument, which I once heard a junior high school principal expound at a public school board meeting: Why worry kids and parents with the stress of trying to do something they are biologically unable to achieve?

This was precisely the outlook Abraham Lincoln had ridiculed in 1859 (see Richard Hofstadter's *Anti-Intellectualism in American Life*); precisely the outlook of Edward Thorndike, inventor of "educational psychology" at Columbia Teachers College; precisely the outlook of H. H. Goddard, chairman of the psychology department at Princeton; precisely the outlook of James Bryant Conant, president of Harvard; precisely the outlook of great private corporate foundations like Rockefeller and Carnegie; precisely the outlook of Charles Darwin and his first cousin, Francis Galton. You can find this point of view active in Plato, in John Calvin, in Benedict (Baruch) Spinoza, in Johann Fichte, and in so many other places it would take a long book to do justice to them.

As long as ordinary Americans like Ben Franklin's dad were in charge of educating their young, America escaped domination from the deadly assumptions of permanent inferiority — whether spiritual, intellectual, or biological — which provide the foundation for rigid social classes, by justifying them. As long as the crazy quilt of libertarian impulses found in the American bazaar prevailed, a period which takes us to the Civil War, America was a place of miracles for ordinary people through self-education. To a fractional degree it still is, thanks to tradition owing nothing to post-WWII government action; but only for those lucky enough to have families which dismiss the assumptions of forced schooling — and hence avoid damage by the weapons of mass instruction.

As the German Method, intended to convert independent Bartleby spirits into human resources, choked off easy escape routes, it wasn't only children who were hurt, but our national prospects. Our founding documents endowed common Americans with rights no government action could alienate, liberty foremost among them. The very label "school" makes a mockery of these rights. We are a worse nation for this radical betrayal visited upon us by generations of political managers masquerading as leaders. And we are a materially poorer nation, as well.

School's structure and algorithms constitute an engine like the little mill that ground salt in the famous fable — long ago it slipped away from anyone's conscious control. It is immune to reform. That's why it must be destroyed. But how?

We will start at the weakest link in the German school chain, the standardized tests which are despised by everyone, school personnel included. The recent past has given us two astonishing accomplishments of citizen action — no, make that three — which should lift your spirits as you prepare to ruin the testing empire — instances of impregnable social fortresses blown to pieces by disorganized, unbudgeted decisions of ordinary people. Call these examples "Bartleby Moments." Think of the ending of the Vietnam War, when young people filled the streets; think of the tearing down of the Berlin Wall; think of the swift dissolution of the Soviet Union.

Bartleby Moments

By the end of WWII, schooling had replaced education in the US, and shortly afterwards, standardized testing became the steel band holding the entire enterprise together. Test scores rather than accomplishment became the mark of excellence as early as 1960, and step by step the public was brought, through various forms of coercion including journalism, to believe that marks on a piece of paper were a fair and accurate proxy for human quality. As Alexander Solzhenitsyn, the Nobel Prize winning Russian author, said, in a *Pravda* article on September 18, 1988, entitled "How to Revitalize Russia:"

> No road for the people [to recover from Communism] will ever be open unless the government completely gives up control over us or any aspect of our lives. It has led the country into an abyss and it does not know the way out.

Break the grip of official testing on students, parents and teachers, and we will have taken the logical first step in revitalizing education. But nobody should believe this step can be taken politically — too much money and power is involved to allow the necessary legislative action; the dynamics of our society tend toward the *creation* of public opinion, not any *response* to it. There is only one major exception to that rule: Taking to the streets. In the past half-century the US has witnessed successful citizen action many times: In the overthrow of the

Jim Crow laws and attitudes; in the violent conclusion to the military action in Vietnam; in the dismissal of a sitting American president from office. In each of these instances the people led, and the government reluctantly followed. So it will be with standardized testing. The key to its elimination is buried inside a maddening short story published in 1853 by Herman Melville: "Bartleby the Scrivener."

I first encountered "Bartleby" as a senior at Uniontown High School, where I was unable to understand what it might possibly signify. As a freshman at Cornell I read it again, surrounded by friendly associates doing the same. None of us could figure out what the story meant to communicate, not even the class instructor.

Bartleby is a human photocopy machine in the days before electro-mechanical duplication, a low-paid, low-status position in law offices and businesses. One day, without warning or explanation, Bartleby begins to exercise free will — he decides which orders he will obey and which he will not. If not, he replies, "I would prefer not to." To an order to participate in a team-proofreading of a copy he's just made, he announces without dramatics, "I would prefer not to." To an order to pop around the corner to pick up mail at the post office, the same: "I would prefer not to." He offers no emotion, no enlargement on any refusal; he prefers not to explain himself. Otherwise, he works hard at copying.

That is, until one day he prefers not to do that, either. *Ever again.* Bartleby is done with copying. But not done with the office which employed him to copy! You see, without the boss' knowledge, he *lives* in the office, sleeping in it after others go home. He has no income sufficient for lodging. When asked to leave that office, and given what amounts to a generous severance pay for that age, he prefers not to leave — and not to take the severance. Eventually, Bartleby is taken to jail, where he prefers not to eat. In time, he sickens from starvation, and is buried in a pauper's grave.

The simple exercise of free will, without any hysterics, denunciations, or bombast, throws consternation into social machinery — free will contradicts the management principle. Refusing to allow yourself to be regarded as a "human resource" is more revolutionary than any revolution on record. After years of struggling with Bartleby, he finally taught me how to break the chains of German Method schooling. It took a half-century for me to understand the awesome instrument each of us has through free will to defeat Germanic schooling, and to destroy the adhesive which holds it together — standardized testing.

Signposts pointing our attention toward the Bartleby power within us are more common than we realize in the global imagination, as Joseph Campbell's splendid works on myth richly demonstrate (as do both Testaments of the Bible), but we needn't reach back very far to discover Thoreau's cornerstone essay on civil disobedience as a living spring in the American imagination, or Gandhi's spectacular defeat of the British Empire through "passive resistance" as bold evidence that as Graham Greene should have taught us by now, "they" would prefer to torture those who expect to be tortured.

Mass abstract testing, anonymously scored, is the torture centrifuge whirling away precious resources of time and money from productive use and routing it into the hands of testing magicians. It happens only because the tormented allow it. Here is the divide-and-conquer mechanism *par excellence*, the wizard-wand which establishes a bogus rank order among the schooled, inflicts prodigies of stress upon the unwary, causes suicides, family breakups, and grossly perverts the learning process — while producing no information of any genuine worth. Testing can't predict who will become the best surgeon, college professor, or taxicab driver; it predicts nothing which would impel any sane human being to enquire after these scores. Standardized testing is very good evidence our national leadership is bankrupt and has been so for a very long time. The two-party system has been unable to give us reliable leadership, its system of campaign finance almost guarantees we get managers, not leaders; I think Ralph Nader has correctly identified it as a single party with two heads — itself bankrupt.

I don't know what to do about that, but I do know how to bring the testing empire to an end, to rip out its heart and make its inventors, proponents, and practitioners into pariahs whose political allies will abandon them.

Let a group of young men and women, one fully aware that these tests add no value to individual lives or the social life of the majority, use the power of the Internet to recruit other young people to refuse, quietly, to take these tests. No demonstrations, no mud-slinging, no adversarial politics — to simply write across the face of the tests placed in front of them, "I would prefer not to take this test." Let no hierarchy of anti-test management form; many should advise the project, but nobody should wrap themselves in the mantle of leadership. The best execution would not be uniform, but would take dozens of different shapes around the country. Like the Congregational Church, there should be no attempt to organize national meetings, although national chatrooms, blogs, and mission-enhancing advisors of all political and philosophical stripes will be welcome. To the extent this project stays unorganized, it cannot help but succeed; to the extent "expert" leadership pre-empts it, it can be counted on to corrupt itself. Think Linux, not Microsoft. Everyone who signs on should get an equal credit, latecomers as well as pioneers. Unto this last should be the watchword.

I prefer not to. Let the statement be heard, at first erratically and then in an irresistible tide, in classrooms across the country. If only one in ten prefer not to, the press will scent an evergreen story and pick up the trail; the group preferring not to will grow like the snowball anticipating the avalanche.

What of the ferocious campaign of intimidation which will be waged against the refuseniks? Retribution will be threatened, scapegoats will be targeted for public humiliation. Trust me, think Alice in Wonderland; the opposition will be a house of cards, the retribution an illusion. Will the refusers be denied admission to colleges? Don't be naïve. College is a business before it's anything else; already a business starving for customers.

The Bartleby Project begins by inviting 60,000,000 American students, one by one, to peacefully refuse to take standardized tests or to participate in any preparation for these tests; it asks *them* to act because adults chained to institutions and corporations are unable to; because these tests pervert education, are disgracefully inaccurate, impose brutal stresses without reason, and actively encourage a class system which is poisoning the future of the nation.[4]

The Bartleby Project should allow no compromise. That will be the second line of defense for management, a standard trick taught in political science seminars. Don't fall for it. Reject compromise. No need to explain why. No need to shout. May the spirit of the scrivener put steel in your backbone. Just say:

I would prefer not to take your test.

An old man's prayers will be with you.

The Bartleby Project was first announced publicly on April 6, 2008, at the 14th Annual International Development Conference at Harvard. It was presented in a formal talk to an audience from the Harvard Graduate School of Education, and then as a statement made to a panel of testing authorities at the Kennedy School of Government.

[4] You'll be in good company. On May 27, 2008, Smith College, the legendary women's college in Northampton, Massachusetts, announced it would no longer require applicants for admission to submit SAT scores. It had become dubious of the validity of standardized tests in predicting success. In future at Smith, the most important criteria for admission will be writing ability, evidence of character and talent, significant extracurricular accomplishment. Schools which have eliminated standardized tests have observed no decline in academic ability.

Index

About the author

John Taylor Gatto taught 30 years in public schools before resigning from school teaching on the op-ed pages of the *Wall Street Journal* during the year he was named New York State's official Teacher of the Year. Since then he has been a tireless advocate for school reform, traveling over three million miles to lecture on the subject. His earlier book, *Dumbing Us Down,* has sold over 100,000 copies.

New Society Publishers

ENVIRONMENTAL BENEFITS STATEMENT

New Society Publishers has chosen to produce this book on recycled paper made with **100% post consumer waste**, processed chlorine free, and old growth free.

For every 5,000 books printed, New Society saves the following resources:[1]

24	Trees
2,188	Pounds of Solid Waste
2,408	Gallons of Water
3,140	Kilowatt Hours of Electricity
3,978	Pounds of Greenhouse Gases
17	Pounds of HAPs, VOCs, and AOX Combined
6	Cubic Yards of Landfill Space

[1]Environmental benefits are calculated based on research done by the Environmental Defense Fund and other members of the Paper Task Force who study the environmental impacts of the paper industry.

NEW SOCIETY PUBLISHERS